# He That Speaks From Heaven

KEVIN ETTA JR

# DEDICATION

This book is dedicated to: "the city of the living God, the heavenly Jerusalem, and to an innumerable company of angels… To the general assembly and church of the firstborn, which are written in heaven; and to God the Judge of all; and to the spirits of just men made perfect. And to Jesus the mediator of the new covenant; and to the blood of sprinkling, that speaks better things than that of Abel" (Hebrews 12:22-24).

# CONTENTS

# ACKNOWLEDGMENTS

I want to appreciate all the journeyers who have contributed in one way or another to the grace and presence of the LORD in my life. Your faith and/or temptations and trials have brought me to the shores of a rich, fulfilling and constantly evolving spiritual experience in Christ.

## CHAPTER ONE
# A WORD FROM THE LORD

*"How long wilt thou forget me, O LORD? forever?*
*how long wilt thou hide thy face from me? How long*
*shall I take counsel in my soul, having sorrow in my*
*heart daily? how long shall mine enemy be exalted*
*over me? Consider and hear me, O LORD my God:*
*lighten mine eyes, lest I sleep the sleep of death;*
*Lest mine enemy say, I have prevailed against him;*
*and those that trouble me rejoice when I am moved.*
*But I have trusted in thy mercy; my heart shall*
*rejoice in thy salvation. I will sing unto the LORD,*
*because he hath dealt bountifully with me."*
*(Psalm 13:1-6)*

I had spent several months praying for a breakthrough around finances and was in search mode for a new opportunity to open up for me. The general economic climate appeared very bleak, and forecasts by experts were not reassuring. Weeks and months passed and door after door that initially seemed to be on the verge of opening suddenly and unexpectedly closed shut.

Twice, early during this period of waiting and expectation, the Lord appeared to me in a dream and had a conversation with me on different subjects. Each time I was excited upon seeing him and thankful that I had the opportunity of an audience with him. I was expectant that my disappointments and longstanding expectations would finally be addressed. But on both occasions, it was not to be.

On the second of these visits, the Lord was telling me something particular about goings-on in the world, and as He spoke, I waited respectfully for an opening to jump in and talk about my 'need'. But each time I would have jumped in to talk about my issue, the Lord would begin an entirely new strain of the conversation. Again, I waited patiently, trying to be respectful, and just when I would be on the verge of jumping in and interjecting to get him to talk about my problem, He would again veer off in another direction and begin a new conversation.

I began to get very distressed, because I couldn't get the Lord to talk about what I considered my own pressing, longstanding priority. At length, and while I was still trying to find an opening to launch into my own conversation with him, He vanished, and I awoke from the dream!

By now, I was very troubled. The way and manner the Lord behaved in that dream and the way the dream ended with him, by my own understanding, ignoring my pressing need and vanishing without addressing it or allowing me to bring it up – left me wondering whether that was a sign or some kind of signal to me that my expectations would not be fulfilled in that area, or perhaps that things would not open up for me in that vein after all.

I continued in this troubled state of mind for weeks until quite suddenly and without warning things turned around and the opportunity I was waiting for opened up and presented itself to me.

A week after these welcome developments, the Lord again appeared to me in a dream.

In this dream, there appeared to be a gathering of people and the Lord was in the midst. There was great joy at the presence of the Lord and the mood was one of rejoicing.

As I approached and came near to where the Lord stood, I asked him: "Lord how long will you make people wait and wait and wait before you finally answer their prayer and help them?"

Immediately I said that the atmosphere in the room changed, and it initially appeared as if my statement and my words had offended the Lord, who now moved away to another part of the room.

Later the Lord circled back to where I was and asked me why I spoke to him that way and said those things to him. I apologized and explained that I had not intended to offend, but it was just that sometimes one cries and cries and cries – and yet, no answer appears to be forthcoming. I reminded him of how long I had been crying to him about my need and it was only the previous week that I finally got an answer (for which I thanked him then and again thanked him now). But I went on and again reminded him about the last two occasions He appeared and each time I attempted to start a conversation about my need He veered off on a different tangent until, finally, He disappeared.

I told the Lord that I can't help being persistent and tenacious about my conversation and relationship with him and all its facets. But what about others whose faith may not be that way? Who may not be able to stay on point day after day, week after week, month after month? How will they cope? Even if they want to stay on point -- distractions, temptations and other competing obligations may make it near impossible for them to remain steadfast. If things looked so hard for me, how will others who may not have a background and a history that I've had – how will they cope in these circumstances?

In reply, the Lord told me three things He wanted me to share with his people.

**A TIME AND A SEASON**

The first thing the lord told me is that there is a time and a season for every event and until the time appointed arrives the event cannot manifest; it cannot happen. He reminded me of the Scripture in Ecclesiastes 3:1

*"To everything there is a season, and a time to every purpose under the heaven"*

The Lord told me that the reason He appeared to ignore my 'priority' when He spoke with me on the two occasions I recalled is that HE KNEW what was on my mind; HE KNEW I was trying to get his attention; but the time was not yet ripe and so, given my anxiety, He calculated that there was no benefit in broaching the issue with me – because there was nothing He could say that would satisfy my anxiety at that moment. The time for fulfillment of my expectation and request had not come.

**WAIT FOR THE VISION**

Second, the Lord told me to tell his people to learn to wait patiently for the promises of God. He referred me to Habakkuk 2:3;

*"For the vision is yet for an appointed time, but at the end it shall speak, and not lie: though it tarry, wait for it; because it will surely come, it will not tarry."*

The Lord said waiting is naturally something unpleasant, especially when we are seized with a sense of urgency about what we consider to be a priority. But waiting is an opportunity to build our communion and deepen our relationship and intimacy with God through fervent, persistent prayer.

**PUT GOD IN REMEMBRANCE**

The Lord then said that one of the things we must do while we wait for the promises of God is to constantly put him in remembrance about his promises as commanded in the Scriptures:

Isaiah 62:6 - 7

*"I have set watchmen upon thy walls, O Jerusalem, which shall never hold their peace day nor night: ye that make mention of the LORD, keep not silence, And give him no rest, till he establish, and till he make Jerusalem a praise in the earth..."*

*(KJV)*

Another translation renders the verse like this:

*"On your walls, O Jerusalem, I have set watchmen; all the day and all the night they shall never be silent. You who put the Lord in remembrance, take no rest, and give him no rest until he establishes Jerusalem and makes it a praise in the earth."*
*(ESV)*

The Lord said the travail I went through is part of the process of creating life from the spiritual to the physical. For new life to be birthed into this realm there must be a conception and then a gestation and development of the promise of God in us. Faith must take root in us and grow through a life cycle into a manifested or materialized promise of God. In many cases there will be the usual birth pains and travails of delivery as we struggle to materialize the promises of God and answers to prayer in our lives. This is a pattern of spiritual growth and development and the path to spiritual success, victory and triumph that manifests its proofs in the physical.

Of course, there are people who receive answers to prayer that do not necessarily experience these kinds of travail. But my understanding from the Lord is that for many, and perhaps for most, He desires that they plod through this path to build faith in them; to deepen his fellowship and communion with them.

May the Lord grant us wisdom to understand and prosper in all his perfect will. Amen.

## CHAPTER TWO
# THE SECRET PLACE OF GOD

*"He that dwelleth in the secret place of the most High shall abide under the shadow of the Almighty" (Psalm 91:1).*

*"And I saw in the right hand of him that sat on the throne a book written within and on the backside, sealed with seven seals. And I saw a strong angel proclaiming with a loud voice, Who is worthy to open the book, and to loose the seals thereof? And no man in heaven, nor in earth, neither under the earth, was able to open the book, neither to look thereon. And I wept much, because no man was found worthy to open and to read the book, neither to look thereon. And one of the elders saith unto me, Weep not: behold, the Lion of the tribe of Juda, the Root of David, hath prevailed to open the book, and to loose the seven seals thereof" (Revelation 5:1-5).*

The great challenge of our times and in the humdrum of our daily lives is the question of power. I don't refer to physical power or even necessarily the spiritual power to heal the sick or perform miracles. But power in the most basic and atomic sense of who has power and influence with God? When the chips are down and an answer is earnestly needed, who can call upon the Lord and get an answer? And get a response?

We are reminded of the situation in the time of Daniel. King Nebuchadnezzar had a troubling dream, and to resolve the interpretation of it he summoned his wise men and astrologers and demanded of them that they tell him not only the interpretation but the dream itself, first and foremost. Of course, they became very distressed because they could not do what the king had asked. Then Nebuchadnezzar gave them an ultimatum that was essentially a death sentence. Until Daniel intervened.

Upon hearing the ultimatum, Daniel requested that he be given an opportunity to research the matter. He then went home and together with his three comrades prevailed upon God through the night for an answer to the riddle posed by Nebuchadnezzar.

The next day, Daniel walked into the presence of the king and said that the secret had been revealed to him but not because of any wisdom that he personally possessed. But there is a God in Heaven that reveals secrets and He it is that has made known to Nebuchadnezzar what shall be in the latter days.

This personal spiritual triumph for Daniel, answers to the question we asked earlier as to who has power with God. The angel in Revelation 5:2 asked a similar question: *"Who is worthy to open the book [in the hand of He that sits upon the Throne], and to loose the seals thereof."*

Who are those persons that have power to move God's hand when He may not initially appear disposed to a particular course of action? God has a certain amount of inertia in his orientation and dealings with man. When He is moving in a certain direction, He is not naturally inclined to stop or to change course –until He has satisfied himself. Nor is He naturally inclined to move when He is stationary. So, the question becomes: how can we learn to move God? How can we cause him to change course when He may be inclined one way or the other? This brings us to our topic.

## THE SECRET PLACE

Daniel 11:32 says: *"But the people that do know their God shall be strong, and do exploits."*

There is a place where we get the "knowing"; where we get melded together with God. There is a secret place where we become irradiated with God's favor and grace through deep fellowship, communion, and inter-relationship with him. We may not emerge a celebrated miracle worker or with the notoriety of one that has many apparent and openly visible giftings and abilities. But we emerge from his presence a people that have a persistent and embedded state of grace by which we are surrounded with his goodwill and favor.

I recall when the great Prophet Isaiah came to King Hezekiah and said to him: *"Thus saith the LORD, Set thine house in order: for thou shalt die, and not live"* (Isaiah 38:1).

Hezekiah didn't pick a fight with the man of God for giving him a negative message – like some people might be prone to do. Hezekiah didn't whine and complain to others not involved in that matter to rubbish the integrity of the man of God or curry sympathy for himself. He didn't look to men. Rather Hezekiah looked to God and prayed. Hezekiah was able to do this naturally because he knew by way of practical experience the way to the secret place. He went there often. For all intents and purposes that is where he lived. And the Bible holds a promise in Psalm 91:1 that says:

> *"He that dwelleth in the secret place of the most High shall abide under the shadow of the Almighty."*

Reading on down to the end of that Psalm, the Psalmist expands further on what it means to dwell "under the shadow of the Almighty" and describes the various protections, protocols and favors that entail.

Hezekiah was not a prophet. Even if he had been, he was not a prophet like Isaiah. He was no miracle worker like Isaiah. But he dwelt in the secret place of God nonetheless – like Isaiah did. As a result, before Isaiah could exit from the large palace grounds, he heard a Voice from above asking him to turn around and go back. Isaiah obeyed, and when he came again into the presence of the king the Word of the Lord came to him:

> *"Thus saith the Lord: You shall not die but live; I have added 15 more years to your life."*

It is good and proper that we go to the elders of the Church or a man of God for prayer when we are in need, for that is in accordance with the Scriptures. But God's perfect will for us is that we each might be able to find our own way to the secret place where we can get 'credentials' of our own and not always operate under the context of the grace flowing out from another. The secret place is a place of prayer. It is a place of seclusion; not a place where we go to become popular. Popularity will come later (if it must), after we have tarried in the presence of God and got credentials of our own. When we then emerge from the secret place and open our mouths to speak, people will take note and comment like they did when they heard Jesus' disciples speak:

*"Now when they saw the boldness of Peter and John, and perceived that they were unlearned and ignorant men, they marveled; and they took knowledge of them, that they had been with Jesus"* (Acts 4:13).

The secret place is a place of prayer. If you want to be great, then learn how to pray. Learn how to pray and get an answer from God. Learn how to move Heaven, how to overcome the Divine inertia and move God's hand. The Bible says:

*"Elijah was a man of like passions like we are, and he prayed..."* (James 5:17).

It is remarkable that the first we hear about Elijah in the Bible is AFTER he finished praying and emerged from the secret place – not before. That is when he achieved notoriety. Elijah is joined to the Bible narrative by one word, a conjunction: "and".

*"AND Elijah the Tishbite, who was of the inhabitants of Gilead, said unto Ahab, As the LORD God of Israel liveth, before whom I stand, there shall not be dew nor rain these years, but according to my word"* (1 Kings 17:1).

Prior to this moment, we hear nothing about Elijah; not wealth he did or did not inherit; not the schools he did or didn't attend. We hear nothing about his past or history – whether he had succeeded or failed at ventures he had embarked upon. Whether he married or not, etc. All that is relevant from Heaven's standpoint and the standpoint of the Spirit of God is that he emerged from the secret place of prayer and communion with God and bound the future of Israel and its wayward King to his word: *"there shall not be dew nor rain these years EXCEPT BY MY WORD."*

A lot of the things slated to happen at the Second Coming of Christ will only happen when a people arise who know the way and dwell in the secret place of God. As our Lord commanded, these people will pray what we describe as Our Lord's Prayer, which says (among other things):

*"Thy Kingdom come; Thy will be done on earth – as it is in Heaven."*

This is a powerful prayer that will become a way of life for these saints, and they will be instrumental in kicking off that great series of events we know as the Coming of the Lord. These will be simple folks, many of whom may not be household names. But they dwell in the secret place day and night. Some of them may remain largely unknown until, like John the Baptist, they emerge and begin to do exploits – *"And the child grew, and waxed strong in spirit, and was in the deserts till the day of his shewing unto Israel"* (Luke 1:80).

Will you be among that number?

The Grace of our Lord Jesus Christ be with you.

## CHAPTER THREE

# THE NOW GOD

*"That which was from the beginning, which we have heard, which we have seen with our eyes, which we have looked upon, and our hands have handled, of the Word of life; (For the life was manifested, and we have seen it, and bear witness, and shew unto you that eternal life, which was with the Father, and was manifested unto us;) That which we have seen and heard declare we unto you, that ye also may have fellowship with us: and truly our fellowship is with the Father, and with his Son Jesus Christ. And these things write we unto you, that your joy may be full."*
*(1 John 1:1-4)*

One of the great and unique things about the gospel is the fact it is not a set of theories about God or what God does. The Gospel is unique in that it is one big testimony of what and who God is, what He has done and what He will do going forward. It is God brought home to us; God made personal and tangible to us – as in the God we can relate to. A God we can reason with, we can communicate with. A God who is willing and able to save and to deliver. The Gospel is not a chronicle of history; what is past and what is to come. The Gospel is a testament to the Now God; the God who is right here, right now. The God we can touch, and we can experience through fellowship with our Lord Jesus.

**WHILE WE LOOK NOT AT THINGS WHICH ARE SEEN**

Generations removed from the Garden of Eden, we are only now able to recover somewhat of our long-lost identity as sons and daughters of God after the fall. The Scriptures say:

*"For as in Adam all die, even so in Christ shall all be made alive"* (1 Cor. 15:22).

So that having become reborn from above through Christ we are able to begin the process of [self-] discovery and recovery of all that was lost in Adam as to our Divine nature and our understanding and comprehension of it. The Scriptures elsewhere say:

*"Work out your own salvation with fear and trembling"* (Philippians 2:12).

The process of attaining full stature is long and arduous. But it begins with an acceptance of Jesus Christ as Lord and Savior. And then the discovery... that we are spirit beings possessing a soul and dwelling presently in a physical body. This is the construct that exists today, and we labor constantly to bear this unwieldy body and, as Apostle Paul says, "bring it under subjection."

It is hard for us to see clearly through this earthly construct in which we presently dwell. 1 Co. 13:12 says:

*"For now we see through a glass, darkly; but then face to face: now I know in part; but then shall I know even as also I am known"* – and by this we understand that our 'son-ship' is a work in progress.

We see things of the earth all too clearly, but not the things that are from Heaven. We hear things of the earth clearly, but strain to hear the voice that calls to us from above. It becomes so easy for us to relegate the voice of God to the background of our consciousness, because we are not accustomed to it in our earthly construct. Ultimately for many – even among saints – God is not really for the here and now. He belongs in some displaced, far-off period when we shall enter "the sweet by and by" or when the Rapture comes; or the time of the Resurrection.

But no. The challenge is for us to:

*"look not at the things which are seen, but at the things which are not seen: for the things which are seen are temporal; but the things which are not seen are eternal"* (2 Cor. 4:18).

The things which are readily seen, the things that pertain or relate to the environment of this earthly construct, though they appear real and are real within the context native to their existence, are "temporal." That means they are not substantial. They are passing in nature and have no fixed foundation or presence.

Good news: your problem is not substantial. Your difficulty is not substantial. Your predicament has no fixed foundation or presence in your life. It is going to pass. Try not to become too fixated on it, because it is passing. It gains strength and presence the more you focus on it and give it attention. I say "try" because it can be hard given the fact, we are so accustomed to this earthly construct and its way and mannerisms.

But focus rather on the things that are not readily visible or readily seen from an earthly standpoint – *"because the things which are not seen are eternal."* These things have real depth and root, though we don't always realize this due to being more focused on the natural versus the spiritual dynamics. The spiritual dynamics have real depth, real 'thickness' if you will. These things have more of a fixed foundation or presence in our lives, and though we don't often or easily "see" them these are the things that define us. In other words, our physical lives take their 'firmware', design and character from the things that are "not seen."

So, for us to begin to appreciate and see the God who is in the here and now in terms of his demonstrable presence in our lives, we must begin to undergo this subtle and then overt transformation in our perceptions of the heavenly versus the earthly; the spiritual versus the physical. God is the God of Now.

## A NAME ABOVE EVERY NAME

We need to understand the magnitude and caliber of weapons and heavy equipment that we are endowed with if we are going to begin to appreciate and see God in the here and now dimension. What are the heavy weapons and tools that we are bequeathed through Christ? What is that singular, most powerful, universal, and wonderful of weapons that we have in our armory? We know of the universal remote control that is programmed and configured to operate different brands of equipment. We have master keys that can open any door in a facility. What is the universal remote and master key that can open any door, unlock any hold, deflect any missile, parry any blow, and submit any enemy? The Scriptures tell us.

*"Wherefore God also hath highly exalted him, and given him a name which is above every name: That at the name of Jesus every knee should bow, of things in heaven, and things in earth, and things under the earth; And that every tongue should confess that Jesus Christ is Lord"* (Philippians 2:9-11).

We need to be constantly reminded of these things and the fact that: *"Whosoever shall call upon the name of the Lord shall be saved"* (Romans 10:13). Whatever your current situation or circumstances, and regardless of your predicament, call upon the Lord. He himself said: *"Call upon me in the day of trouble: I will deliver you, and you shall glorify me"* (Psalm 50:15).

When you are in trouble is not the time to whine and complain to somebody for the sake of whining and complaining. That's also not the time to give up on God and turn away from him. That's the time, the right time, to call upon him – for He has promised to deliver. It's tempting to do all the other things because we are in the earthly construct. But remember we have to begin to look away from the things that are seen and toward the things that are not seen – because these are the things that have depth, that have root. God has depth. God has a sure foundation. If you trust in him, you will not be moved out from your place.

*"They that trust in the LORD shall be as mount Zion, which cannot be removed"* (Psalm 125:1).

God has his feet firmly planted. He cannot be moved. Trust in him and you will not be put to shame.

## THE KINGDOM OF GOD IS AMONG YOU

God's power is now. God's grace is here now, and you may utilize it by faith. It is not something far off. It is now. It is not something tentative. It is now. It is not a work in progress. It is right now. Our Lord taught these things when He walked the earth. Hear him.

*"And when he was demanded of the Pharisees, when the kingdom of God should come, he answered them and said, The kingdom of God cometh not with observation: Neither shall they say, Lo here! or, lo there! for, behold, the kingdom of God is within you" (Luke 17:20-21).*

The Jews reasoned very much the same way Christians in our day reason. Because of their little faith they always considered God's power in terms of "When." But Jesus corrected them and taught God's power in terms of "Now." He taught that the Kingdom of God is in your midst. It's among you, it's all around you – all you must do is tap into it by faith. All you must do is speak the word.

*"Say not in thine heart, Who shall ascend into heaven? (that is, to bring Christ down from above:) Or, Who shall descend into the deep? (that is, to bring up Christ again from the dead.) But what saith it? The word is nigh thee, even in thy mouth, and in*

*thy heart: that is, the word of faith, which we preach; That if thou shalt confess with thy mouth the Lord Jesus, and shalt believe in thine heart that God hath raised him from the dead, thou shalt be saved. For with the heart man believeth unto righteousness; and with the mouth confession is made unto salvation. For the scripture saith, Whosoever believeth on him shall not be ashamed" (Romans 10:6-11).*

## I AM THE RESURRECTION AND THE LIFE

Our Lord came up against the same mindset with those that were closest to him. Hear him as He talked with Martha about the untimely death of her brother Lazarus.

*"Then said Martha unto Jesus, Lord, if thou hadst been here, my brother had not died. But I know, that even now, whatsoever thou wilt ask of God, God will give it thee. Jesus saith unto her, Thy brother shall rise again. Martha saith unto him, I know that he shall rise again in the resurrection at the last day. Jesus said unto her, I am the resurrection, and the life: he that believeth in me, though he were dead, yet shall he live: And whosoever liveth and believeth in me shall never die. Believest thou this?" (John 11: 21-26).*

So, first Martha laments that Jesus was not on hand in Lazarus' final hours and to that Jesus says: "Thy brother shall rise again." Martha replies, "Oh, yes; yes, I know he will rise again at the Resurrection in the last day." Jesus responds with: "No, no, not then. But right NOW. I AM THE RESURRECTION and THE LIFE. Believe me right now. Now, not tomorrow. Right now.

What do you want from God today? What is your heart's desire? Better yet – what do you need from God? For what does your heart yearn and waste away in exasperation? Why don't you begin to ask what you will right now? You say: "Well I've been asking all this time…" We're not talking about that; about what you've been doing. We're talking about what you're going to do right now. Several times in the Gospels people prayed to the Lord for help and when He turned around to meet them face to face He would say: "Ask what I shall give to you" or "Ask what I should do for you." God is on point with your faith in the here and now. So, ask him RIGHT NOW. He is the NOW GOD, and He wants to be that Person for you RIGHT NOW that you are on point with your faith.

He is the Now God.

The Grace of our Lord Jesus Christ be with you.

## CHAPTER FOUR
# JESUS IS COMING

*"So Christ was once offered to bear the sins of many; and unto them that look for him shall he appear the second time without sin unto salvation"*
*(Hebrews 9:28).*

In every instance where our Lord talked about his return, or where it has been spoken of by the first apostles, it is spoken of in terms of a glorious Coming -- if you like, a glorious Homecoming where our Lord is reunited with his family; with his Saints, and at which time He bestows upon them ascendant and transcendent gifts and powers that He carries with him to this glorious "Supper." Various metaphors and types have been used in the Scriptures to describe this Homecoming, such as supper, feast, gathering- unto-him, glorified-in-his-saints, manifestation-of-the-sons-of-God, etc. And it is generally presented as a time of unprecedented upliftment, ecstasy, empowerment, promotion and rejoicing in the Lord's Coming and Presence.

## THE JOY OF THE LORD

In a vision I had of the Lord's Coming, I saw the Saints become literally transformed by the sense, knowledge, and awareness that "Jesus is in town." I will never forget that vision and the power of it. People from all walks of life who had been otherwise crestfallen, downtrodden, seemingly hopeless, or just hanging on or hanging in there – or persisting and persevering in the worship and service of the Lord – were transformed by their perception and capacity to intuit, to see, and to experience the "sign" of our Lord's return whereby they knew Jesus was "in town." They were empowered, they were energized, they were united (who had captured or caught the vision of this "sign") in their faith, worship, and purpose and they rallied publicly and openly for Jesus. I didn't see any of the denominational divides or banners that are so evident today. I didn't hear people arguing and drawing lines in the sand to separate themselves among different groupings based on interpretative differences and nuances of doctrine (that all sides generally hold to be true and fundamental anyway). All I saw was a people empowered and energized – a people who suddenly were able to see through a different lens into a new universe of spiritual realities and glorious possibilities.

When I beheld this effervescing and almost tumultuous joy being evident in the saints, I began to realize even more what the Scriptures meant when they say in Nehemiah 8:10 that: *"The joy of the Lord is your Strength."* Because the joy of these Believers that caught this vision (or this sign or whatever we might call it) WAS MAKING THEM STRONG -- SPIRITUALLY STRONG AND IN THE MOMENT!

There are also the words of David in Psalm 28:7 that bear on this moment and this hour of spiritual strength and rapture: *"The LORD is my strength and my shield; my heart trusted in him, and I am helped: therefore my heart greatly rejoiceth; and with my song will I praise him."*

And there is our main Scripture text from Hebrews 9:28 which says:

*"So Christ was once offered to bear the sins of many; and unto them that look for him shall he appear the second time without sin unto salvation."*

The International Standard Version (ISV) casts it in this way: *"so the Messiah was sacrificed once to take away the sins of many people. And he will appear a second time, not to deal with sin, but to bring salvation to those who eagerly wait for him."*

Awesome. To bring salvation to those who eagerly wait for him. Of course, the saints are already 'saved.' So, it is talking here about bringing the saints to the full complement of their salvation in Christ; to full investiture; to a full inheritance and a public attestation and manifestation of that salvation – with all its perks, capabilities and giftings. This explains why the Saints will be rapturously joyful at Jesus' return, because it will signal their coming to Power: their coming into the full value, import and exercise of their inheritance in Christ. But the key phrase and component here is: *"those who eagerly wait for him."* The KJV said: *"unto them that look for him shall he appear..."* So, there is no question but that only to those who live constantly in the 'moment' of his return – who look for him – shall He appear;

shall He give the sign; shall He bring to full salvation and to the complement of the full stature of Christ. Those that live their lives in anticipation and expectation of the Lord. Those for whom Christ is not just and not simply a teaching, a doctrine, or fellowship and involvement in their Church congregation –but those for whom Christ is a life. Is a way of life, a reason for life, a roadmap for life and a vision for life. Like Paul, when he remarked in Philippians 12:2: *"For me to live is Christ..."*

## THE PERSON AND THE PRESENCE

What does it mean to eagerly wait? Or to earnestly wait? Does it mean we do nothing –but wait for the Lord's return? Elsewhere and in different circumstances, our Lord spoke of the Resurrection, what we typically imagine or conceptualize as an event in time, in this manner: *"I am the resurrection and the life"* (John 11:25). Resurrection is a person, not an event. And those that truly believe in the Resurrection (the Person) shall experience the joys of the resurrection (the experience). Similarly, the Coming of the Lord, more than being an event in time is at its core the full realization, full accommodation, and full embrace of the person of Jesus Christ in all of his Glory (his glorious power, his glorious hosts, his glorious train and other glorious parts) in the lives of those Believers who are sanctified by living a life of eagerly expecting Jesus. So that waiting for the Lord's return, becomes a life of constantly looking to Jesus for guidance daily and governance daily as we progressively move and grow through the challenges, commitments, obligations, and responsibilities of this life.

Isaiah also bears on this in his words:

*"Behold, God is my salvation; I will trust, and not be afraid: for the LORD JEHOVAH is my strength and my song; he also is become my salvation"* (Isaiah 12:2).

We see here that God HIMSELF is our salvation. Jehovah HIMSELF is our strength and our song, and He HIMSELF will become our Salvation at his Appearing. So being in the presence of the Presence at his Coming begins to take on a clearer meaning and import.

The Saints of God will experience rapture in every sense of the word, because they will no more be walking on earthly ground than Moses was when he was met by God in the mount and commanded to: *"take off the shoes from your feet, for the ground upon which you walk is holy."* Moses was no longer walking on earthly ground or ground limited and defined by the perceptions, laws, and circumstances of this earthly realm. From the moment Moses saw the "sign" of the burning bush and "turned aside to see this great sight" he began to walk on a Heavenly ground that existed in an altogether different context of realities and opportunities that the Presence of God on that mount made possible.

Similarly, when the Saints of God begin to see the 'sign' of his Coming and become caught up by this they will no longer be on this earthly realm for all intents and purposes --but will begin to walk on Holy ground; on Heavenly ground that has been sanctified by the Lord's Presence and his manifesting Kingdom Authority. You can read the Transfiguration account into this as well; when our Lord took his three disciples into a mount aside and became transfigured before them and there appeared with him Moses and Elijah in a glorified state making conversation with Jesus. During this experience, the disciples no longer 'walked' on this earth for all intents and purposes –but had become elevated by their presence before the Presence of God. And Peter, not fully realizing this, continued to talk about earthly arrangements that were inconsistent with the present context of their unfolding experience, and so the Voice came from God interrupting Peter and admonishing him to pay attention – because he now walked on ground which was holy, which was heavenly (see Matthew 17:5 and Mark 9:7).

**WAITING FOR THE LORD**

Waiting for our Lord doesn't denote an immobility or inactivity of any sort. Rather it is a very active exercise of looking to him. Hebrews 9:28 begins with the words: *"Unto them that look to him…"* Isaiah 62:1 opens up with this very theme of actively looking for the Lord to 'move' in our lives and in the lives of others:

*"For Zion's sake will I not hold my peace, and for Jerusalem's sake I will not rest, until the righteousness thereof go forth as brightness, and the salvation thereof as a lamp that burneth."*

It even uses the words: *"I will not rest, until"* … i.e. until something happens. And this is the same sense brought out when our Lord enjoined us to actively pray: *"Thy Kingdom come; thy will be done in earth, as it is in heaven."* There is nothing passive about that. And so, our attitude of eagerly waiting for the Lord involves an active participation in the effort to 'move' the hand of God; to cause the Lord to move forward in his plans; to accelerate and bring to fruition and ripening all his good will for us. It is line with this that we are told in Daniel 11:32:

*"But the people that do know their God shall be strong, and do exploits."*

And in Isaiah 40:31: *"But they that wait upon the LORD shall renew their strength; they shall mount up with wings as eagles; they shall run, and not be weary; and they shall walk, and not faint."*

## A PEOPLE OF FAITH

Our Lord Jesus was very particular about his Second Coming and being assured in the knowledge that when He returns, He will find a people who are earnestly looking for his return; i.e. a people who have a practicing habit and ongoing lifestyle of looking and surrendering to his dynamic governance and direction in their day-to-day lives —as opposed to just having the "Second Coming" among their articles of faith or stated doctrine or creed.

In Luke 18:1-8 He tells a parable about an unapproachable and ungodly judge who regards no man's person and of whom all are weary. He juxtaposed the unapproachable judge's profile with that of a lowly widow who had none to avenge her – but this judge. The widow appeals to the judge unrelentingly day and night, and for sure the judge is naturally disdainful and dismissive of her. Until at length the judge reasons within himself that even though he fears not God or man, yet this woman's persistence is wearing on him to the point that he might as well just give her what she wants and be at rest. And the judge does just that. Now, before we touch on our Lord's remarks and the lesson of the parable, bear in mind the unspoken inference here is that better people, and more highly placed than this widow, had appealed to this judge —and got no relief. But this lowly woman with few if any credentials, did —because she was persistent; because she conducted her appeal to the judge as a lifestyle-habit and practice; i.e. she had 'faith.' Our Lord enjoins us to be likeminded in prayer and habit towards God and finally asks the crucial question: *"Nevertheless when the Son of man cometh, shall he find faith on the earth?"*

Indeed, shall our Lord find such a habit and lifestyle of faith in us towards God as existed in that lowly woman towards the unapproachable judge? The answer to this question answers to the bigger question of whether we – as Christians and Believers – are ready for our Lord's return.

**REJOICE ALWAYS**

When you read the epistles, and in particular the epistles of Paul, you get the distinct flavor of hearts and minds that --in the midst of disappointments, trials, and tribulations —are warmed by the love of Christ at their very core and the firmly embedded admiration of our Lord and expectation of the glories that will become the possession of the Saints at his Coming. These men suffered serious deprivations and challenges. They suffered challenges also to their faith and work for God. But in and through it all their hearts never grow cold. Their hearts are constantly warmed by their vision, understanding and knowledge of the glories that await them – if they can but hold on to the assurance of their faith until the very end. Have you caught somewhat of a vision of the glories of this inheritance in Jesus Christ? In Ephesians 1:15 -23 Paul prayed earnestly that those who hadn't caught such a vision might catch one. You will need it to keep your heart 'warm' until the end.

In closing, I would like to present what, to many, will be a familiar verse of Scripture but which captures the essence of the warmness, the expectant joys, and the hopes of the first apostles and the elect of all ages to greater and lesser degrees.

*"But what things were gain to me, those I counted loss for Christ. Yea doubtless, and I count all things but loss for the excellency of the knowledge of Christ Jesus my Lord: for whom I have suffered the loss of all things, and do count them but dung, that I may win Christ, And be found in him, not having mine own righteousness, which is of the law, but that which is through the faith of Christ, the righteousness which is of God by faith: That I may know him, and the power of his resurrection, and the fellowship of his sufferings, being made conformable unto his death; If by any means I might attain unto the resurrection of the dead.*

*Not as though I had already attained, either were already perfect: but I follow after, if that I may apprehend that for which also I am apprehended of Christ Jesus. Brethren, I count not myself to have apprehended: but this one thing I do, forgetting those things which are behind, and reaching forth unto those things which are before, I press toward the mark for the prize of the high calling of God in Christ Jesus. Let us therefore, as many as be perfect, be thus minded: and if in anything ye be otherwise minded, God shall reveal even this unto you. Nevertheless, whereto we have already attained, let us walk by the same rule, let us mind the same thing.*

*Brethren, be followers together of me, and mark them which walk so as ye have us for an ensample. (For many walk, of whom I have told you often, and now tell you even weeping, that they are the enemies of the cross of Christ: Whose end is destruction, whose God is their belly, and whose glory is in their shame, who mind earthly things.) For our conversation is in heaven; from whence also we look for the Saviour, the Lord Jesus Christ: Who shall change our vile body, that it may be fashioned like unto his glorious body, according to the working whereby he is able even to subdue all things unto himself" (Philippians 3:7-21).*

# CHAPTER FIVE
# PRINCIPLES OF PRAYER

*"After this manner therefore pray ye: Our Father which art in heaven, Hallowed be thy name. Thy kingdom come. Thy will be done in earth, as it is in heaven. Give us this day our daily bread. And forgive us our debts, as we forgive our debtors. And lead us not into temptation, but deliver us from evil: For thine is the kingdom, and the power, and the glory, forever. Amen" (Matthew 6:9-13).*

Our Lord was emphatic that we ought always to pray and not be fainthearted or weary. He was also emphatic that when we pray, we should expect to be heard; we should expect to get an answer from God. Finally, Jesus was very particular about *how* we pray, to achieve the desired results.

Many prayers are made just for the sake of praying, and if you read the verses preceding our Scripture text above you will see the Lord denouncing loudly various forms of prayer that He considered superfluous and, in some cases, vainglorious. Jesus tells us plainly that the people who pray those forms of prayer have already received their reward, because they have been noticed and celebrated by men —which is what they ultimately desired when they prayed: to be seen and heard of men, by peers, etc. They and their prayers will not be heard by God, and they will not get an answer since they were not praying to God in truth, but used the appearance of prayer to God as a pretext to advance their ulterior and hidden motives which were to be heard and seen by men.

In other cases, it is not so simple. People have prayed, sometimes fervently, and have not received an answer from God. They have not heard back from God and that which they prayed for does not appear to be forthcoming. Sometimes even when it appeared that their prayers were heard and would be answered, ultimately, they linger and linger until they are forgotten. Nothing seems to be forthcoming from the efforts of the persistent supplicant. There seem to be some obstacles, some hidden mechanisms wrestling against the manifestation of that which for the most part God had initially appeared pleased to do.

Our Lord was very resolute about the need, the purpose, and the reward of prayer. He constantly extolled the principle of rewards accruing from prayer. He used several parables to enjoin and exhort the saints toward persistent prayer. He persuaded us through many words that the Holy Father is pleased to answer us when we call out to him, just as an earthly father is happy to give his child bread or some good gift rather than an evil gift. Jesus took time to teach us how to pray and we will be looking at some principles that stand out from his teaching about prayer.

**OUR FATHER WHO ART IN HEAVEN**

To whom do we first look when we are seized by the urge to cry out and appeal for help, for succor? To whom are our eyes first directed when we are beaten down by temptation and trial and things don't seem to be going our way? And beyond the question of whom –where are our eyes drawn and in what direction? For many it is natural that when they are in trouble or become otherwise upset their attentions are drawn and directed to earthly benefactors: wives are drawn to husbands, children are drawn to their parents and guardians, etc. – and this is natural. But beyond the natural order of things, when all is closing in on us where are our attentions typically directed? Psalm 121:1 says: *"I will lift up my eyes unto the hills, from whence cometh my help"*.

When Daniel was being persecuted in Babylon, we are told he retired into his chambers, orientated his gaze toward Jerusalem, the symbol of God's throne and presence, and prayed. In Acts of the Apostles, when Stephen was being stoned, we are told he looked unto the heavens and saw Jesus standing at the right hand of God.

So, back to our question: where does our gaze naturally turn when we are tried and tempted? Does it turn to God or to men? In the first instance, our prayer will be more impactful and potent when our relationship with God is true and strong. When our 'roots' in God are strong, our prayer will be strong. And so, the first question we need to ask ourselves and answer is: how true and how strong is my relationship with God? Have you surrendered your life to Jesus as your Lord and Savior and embraced the salvation which is in Christ? If not, you should do so.

God hears the prayer of those who have not believed in Christ *("That ye may be the children of your Father which is in heaven: for he maketh his sun to rise on the evil and on the good, and sendeth rain on the just and on the unjust" - Matt 5:45)*. But He hears the prayer of his own children better *("And it shall come to pass, that before they call, I will answer; and while they are yet speaking, I will hear" - Isaiah 65:24)*.

If you are a Believer in Christ, how strong are your roots in God? Have you used your time as a Believer being a perpetual juvenile averse to growth and development? Are you growing in the knowledge and wisdom of God? Do you realize that when a child refuses to grow he has little honor? In many instances when there is a lack of growth it is attributable to two things: there is stuntedness and malformation or an outright refusal to develop – and neither case is desirable.

Have you rather used your time in the backwoods of your Christian life (i.e., away from the public view) like David in the Old Testament and Stephen in the New, building and exercising your spiritual muscles in anticipation for that time and that moment when you shall be called upon to play your part in the unfolding agenda of the Gospel and of the Kingdom of God? If you have done this, then you will naturally lift your eyes to

35

Heaven and call out to him as you properly should. If you have not, then you should reflect upon your life and reconsider.

**THY KINGDOM COME**

This represents a very confrontational and aggressive stance. In Matt. 12:28 Jesus said: *"But if I cast out devils by the Spirit of God, then the kingdom of God is come unto you."* Or to paraphrase: "When the Kingdom of God comes down, devils are cast out by the Spirit of God." The Kingdom of God is not first and foremost a city you can see with your eyes and define in terms of space and depth. In Luke 17:20 Jesus taught this way:

*"And when he was demanded of the Pharisees, when the kingdom of God should come, he answered them and said, The kingdom of God cometh not with observation: Neither shall they say, Lo here! or, lo there! for, behold, the kingdom of God is within you."*

His words not mine. A different version than the KJV, the ISV renders it like this: *"Once Jesus was asked by the Pharisees when the kingdom of God would come. He answered them, "The kingdom of God is not coming with a visible display. People won't be saying, 'Look! Here it is!' or 'There it is!' because now the kingdom of God is among you."*

Clearly, our Lord taught that the Kingdom of God is first and foremost a regime or wave of power that manifests itself around any who pray fervently in the Spirit. And so, by calling on the Kingdom of God to come down you are inadvertently calling warring angels to come to your aid and there is war in heaven when this happens (see Revelation 12:7-8 and Luke 10:17-

20). This is a prayer and a creed that will be adopted by a chosen band of prophetic Believers in the end-times. Their faith and prayers will be a precursor to the return of our Lord in glory. These are the elect whose prayers are spoken of as shortening the Tribulation period and ultimately hastening our Lord's return:

*"And except those days should be shortened, there should no flesh be saved: but for the elect's sake those days shall be shortened"* (Matt 24:22).

Thy Kingdom Come is a prayer posture and a prayer disposition to aggressively assail the powers that hold sway in our lives at any given moment.

**THY WILL BE DONE IN EARTH**

Thy will be done in earth, as it is in heaven. What earth? The earth is your life and mine —here in this house of clay, this physical realm. You want God's will to be done in your life in accordance with his original purpose and destiny established in Heaven. The Bible says:

*"Forever, O LORD, thy word is settled in heaven"*

(Psalm 119:89).

God has an original plan and purpose for each one of us in Heaven, an original imprint. The U.S. Treasury and its departments (U.S. mint and Bureau of Engraving and Printing) have the engraving plates for producing U.S. money. Think of what would happen if the engraving plates were compromised, how that might affect the integrity of U.S. legal tender. For many of us, this is somewhat what has happened. The original plan and purpose for our lives has been marred and things are not going as God originally intended. In Jeremiah 29:11 our Lord said:

*"For I know the thoughts that I think toward you, saith the LORD, thoughts of peace, and not of evil, to give you an expected end."*

However, despite this declaration, for many the opposite seems to be the norm. Things appear to be in a state of disrepair and disorder.

We need to appeal to God to enforce, adopt and apply the original imprint and image that He has in his possession to our lives here on earth, to rectify these discrepancies and malformations in our life experiences. That is the line of prayer and the posture of this prayer. When God copies a new image to our lives things begin to take shape. This image copying is a process; it is not all at once —because we are never in a constant state of optimal spiritual, physical, and mental reception. But as we yield to God daily, He applies those "updates" like the way Windows Updates are applied to a PC that is in the appropriate state to receive the updates without interruption. This process will gradually roll us forward to a state of consistency with the original plan, purpose, and schedule of our Divine destiny, a state of spiritual and physical prosperity.

**GIVE US OUR DAILY BREAD**

This is self-explanatory. We should not fail or neglect to ask God for those things that we need. He knows already, but we are expected to ask him. It is a matter of respect, reverence, and intimacy that we do this, and reinforces and strengthens our bonding with him as a benevolent Father.

*"Casting all your care upon him; for he careth for you"*
*(1 Peter 5:7)*

*"Be careful for nothing; but in everything by prayer and supplication with thanksgiving let your requests be made known unto God" (Philippians 4:6).*

*"But my God shall supply all your need according to his riches in glory by Christ Jesus" (Philippians 4:19).*

**FORGIVE OUR TRESPASSES**

It is imperative that we maintain a good relationship with God. Obviously one of things that can impair this relationship is sin and transgression against God. This comes and happens in various and diverse forms we need not enumerate. We all know what this means and how we individually stack up daily. We need to ensure that these breaches are repaired sooner rather than later, so that the enemy does not take undue advantage of the fact we are temporarily "out of service" as it were.

*"My little children, these things write I unto you, that ye sin not. And if any man sin, we have an advocate with the Father, Jesus Christ the righteous: And he is the propitiation for our sins: and not for ours only, but also for the sins of the whole world" (1 John 2:2).*

Just as important as pleading forgiveness for our sins and transgressions against God is learning to forgive and forgiving others. Those two go hand in hand, hence our Lord tied them together when he admonished us about pleading forgiveness in prayer. If we do not forgive others, then we have no basis to ask forgiveness of God, and neither will God forgive us.

## LEAD US NOT INTO TEMPTATION BUT DELIVER US FROM EVIL

Some teach a message that pretty much says that as Christians we ought not expect or experience temptation. Now, temptation is only temptation when it is real, when it happens. Which means bad things can and do happen to God's people. In fact, they are more prone to happen because we are the apple of God's eye, and his archenemy Satan is out to get at God by touching those He loves. Sometimes Satan himself goes to God and gets permission from God to tempt us. In other words, we become the subject of a bet or contest between God and Satan, to see whose bet will come out on top.

A good example of this is the story of Job in the Bible. Our Lord knew this, which is why He prayed in the Gospels at the garden of Gethsemane: *"Father if it be possible, let this cup pass from me; nevertheless not what I wilt, but what thou wilt."* He taught us to do the same thing and to be cognizant of the same dangers and perils when He said to pray: *"And lead us not into temptation"* – and we must teach others no less. Temptation will come, no doubt. Trouble will come, no doubt. Satan's job is to go to and fro seeking whom he may devour. That's his job. Our job is to learn to parry and deflect his blows before they impact us, and if they make impact to endure whilst still calling upon God for deliverance and victory.

The flip side to that prayer is: *"deliver us from evil."* Again, make no mistake: there is evil afoot. People that teach otherwise are not helping the Believers. They are not helping them to be informed about Satan's devices. You know a PC's antivirus software must constantly update its virus definitions to keep abreast of the latest threats. Paul says something similar when in 2 Corinthians 2:11 he said: *"Lest Satan should get an advantage of us: for we are not ignorant of his devices."*

When we fervently pray that the Lord should deliver us from the plans of the evil one, we may begin to have experiences (some, dreams; some, others) that present a graphic display or picture of evil plans or plots against us. Don't be alarmed; this is usually a sign that God is weeding them out and discarding them —but keep praying so that He will finish and complete the work. The worst thing is to not sustain the prayer over a period so God can finish his work, because when that happens things may not only return to the way they were —they can even become worse.

## THINE IS THE KINGDOM, THE POWER AND GLORY

Yes, this is reverent acknowledgement of the fact that our God can accomplish all these things and the victory and justice we seek from him will be wrought because He is God: He is the Almighty God; in Heaven, on earth and under the earth – and there is none other. Our Lord Jesus announced boldly: *"All power is given unto me in heaven and in earth"* (Matt 28:18). And so, we add to our prayer the words: *"In the Name of Jesus"*, so that his Name might encapsulate our prayer as it ascends to the Throne of God.

This is our heritage. We are a glorious people. 1 Peter 2:9 affirms: *"But ye are a chosen generation, a royal priesthood, an holy nation, a peculiar people; that ye should shew forth the praises of him who hath called you out of darkness into his marvelous light."*

The grace of our Lord Jesus Christ be with you.

## CHAPTER SIX
# THE UNIVERSAL REMOTE

*"For I am not ashamed of the gospel of Christ: for it is the power of God unto salvation to everyone that believeth; to the Jew first, and also to the Greek"*
*(Romans 1:16).*

One of the great needs of our times and one that is increasingly contemporary with the times is the need for an identity. People everywhere are desperately searching for something to which to belong. There is the sometimes unspoken and sometimes spoken and demonstrable desire and quest for friendships, for peers, for partnering, for grouping. Sometimes this is evident in our conversations with one another, or you hear it in public discourse on TV, on social media and the Internet: everyone is in some kind of struggle for an identity, or some measure or metric --be it by grouping or association or what not -- by which they can feel cast in a certain mold or identity and are standardized by a peer mechanism or grouping.

We are also witness to the fact that this is demonstrated through homecomings, etc. when families or alumni meet by scheduled and sometimes non-scheduled events to revive and relive their commonalities, associations, and relationships towards this same end: we need to know who we are, and sometimes knowing who we are is accomplished and reinforced through these quests to be identified and have a sense of belonging to something more than just us. We seek to be defined by the group; we desire to be measured by the association. We want to part of a standardized form, and not be seen as a floater without definition. We've created a system of labels and tags to organize ourselves into different social and political groupings for easier differentiation and demagoguery.

The result of our diligence in undertaking these multi-faceted quests is that we are more socially, racially, politically, economically, and spiritually fragmented and polarized today than at any time in history. Even within Christendom, there is acute fragmentation based on different interpretations of doctrine, practice, and tradition on the one hand and institutional rivalries on the other. Christendom as a global unit has not demonstrated a unitary approach for providing the identity we all desire, overtly or covertly; outwardly or inwardly.

However, there is one universal denominator; one universal remote control; one universal factor that can accomplish the goal of providing us with an identity. This is a tool for empowerment, vision, strengthening, encouraging, engendering fellowship and commonality, and advancing the oneness and unity of purpose that is at the foundation of every identity structure. It transcends race, culture, or ethnicity. The universal remote is the Gospel of Jesus Christ.

The Gospel is a spiritual tool and energizer that is not about private interpretations or doctrinal biases. The Gospel is not about race, culture, politics or economic preference or inclination. The Gospel of Jesus Christ is atomic in nature and in its presentation of the Hope that is in Christ; the hope of salvation; the hope of emancipation; the hope of citizenship; the hope of empowerment; the hope of healing and restoration.

There is an interesting illustration of this in Acts 14:6-10: -

*"They were ware of it, and fled unto Lystra and Derbe, cities of Lycaonia, and unto the region that lieth round about: And there they preached the gospel. And there sat a certain man at Lystra, impotent in his feet, being a cripple from his mother's womb, who never had walked: The same heard Paul speak: who stedfastly beholding him, and perceiving that he had faith to be healed, Said with a loud voice, Stand upright on thy feet. And he leaped and walked."*

There is something infinitely inspiring about that verse of Scripture. At this event, Paul was not arguing or debating doctrine, which he occasionally would from time to time depending on the place and the moment. He wasn't settling disputes or trying to resolve doubts and questions among brethren or would-be Believers. The Bible very simply says he preached the Gospel. He preached the Gospel. And that was it.

Of course, he preached the Gospel several times in different places, and so did others.

But the unique thing about this event was that there sat a man who was a cripple. Whose situation was hopeless. This man listened to Paul preach the Gospel and something in the words of Paul and the Gospel Paul preached sounded so hopeful, so optimistic, that this man began to believe that he could be healed, that this atomic message of hope, recovery and repair was somehow meant for him in the here and now —not tomorrow, but right now. He believed the Gospel presented opportunities and prospects that he could cash in on right now —all he needed to do was endorse one of many open checks the message was making available to him. We are told that Paul saw and sensed this. Paul saw that this man was ready to endorse a check right there, right now —and Paul gave him a gentle push to make him do it: *"[Paul] stedfastly beholding him, and perceiving that he had faith to be healed, Said with a loud voice, Stand upright on thy feet. And he leaped and walked."* Praise God.

You see, men have made the Gospel a tussle between my Church and your Church; my Ministry and your Ministry; my Group and your Group. Some have even gone as far as to introduce an ethnic, nationalistic flavor to the Gospel. Exploiting it for political purposes. So that ultimately the "gospel" has become less than desirable for many and discouraged many more. Whereas the Gospel is Power. The Gospel is Hope. The Gospel is Salvation. The Gospel is Favor. The Gospel is Abundant Life. It is empowerment for the racially depressed. The Gospel is empowerment for the socially repressed. It is power for the economically downtrodden. The Gospel presents hope to those who have lost hope in political systems and the general system and purport of governance locally and universally.

The Gospel is the power of God unto all who believe; be they Jew or Greek; Black or White; Hispanic or Oriental, etc. The Gospel cannot be taken hostage by any earthly, man-made grouping, cause, or agenda. The Gospel is atomic and universal at the same time. It is both unique and generic.

The Gospel of Jesus Christ is an offer of citizenship --with the rights that accompany –in a Greater Commonwealth with limitless opportunities and possibilities. When we understand the Gospel and are not just 'religious proponents' --and present it properly -- we create life in people. We generate faith in people. Miracles happen not because we necessarily are endowed with gifts of working miracles, but because we preach and present a message that at its very core is a pressurized capsule of hope, which when burst by the keen interest of the hearer creates a faith that produces breakthrough changes and interventions in their lives. Miracles happen when we present or preach the Gospel of Jesus Christ.

The greatest, most revolutionary, and most explosive and dynamic instrument of change and transformation ever released into the universe was and is the Gospel of Jesus Christ. It presents hope to those in need of social and spiritual identity. It provides a sense of belonging and ownership to the destitute. It provides the hope of general health and wellness to the infirm. It provides the promise of resurrection and glorious life eternal with Jesus to those that embrace it.

When I fellowship with ministers and pastors, one of the things I share with them is that if your message is one that you can only convey to one Church group or one Church organization or denomination, then chances are you are not preaching the Gospel of Jesus Christ. You must come to a point in your relationship with Christ, in your understanding of the Gospel and in your message, where you can effectively communicate and present your message to most any Church organization – indeed, to any Grouping at all -- and still get the message of Christ across. That is when you know you are getting warm in your understanding of the Gospel. If your message will only fit within the confines of one grouping, then chances are you're not really preaching the Gospel but a fragmentation of it. Paul could speak and communicate to anyone in any grouping of people. He himself said: *"I am all things to all men, that I might by all means save some"* (1 Corinthians. 9:22). For Paul, this did not mean all would accept the message (nor does it mean that for us). But it meant he was able to communicate to them. He was able to talk to them. The Gospel has something for everyone. It speaks to everyone. It speaks to every ethnicity. It speaks to every race. It speaks to every condition. It speaks to every situation. It speaks to every power –high or low, great or small. It is a universal remote control.

*"For I am not ashamed of the gospel of Christ: for it is the power of God unto salvation to every one that believeth; to the Jew first, and also to the Greek"*

I pray that we may continue to meditate on these things and that the Lord will grant us the wisdom and the courage to do his bidding in accordance with all his Divine will. Amen.

## CHAPTER SEVEN
# BY MY SPIRIT

*"And the angel that talked with me came again, and waked me, as a man that is wakened out of his sleep, And said unto me, What seest thou? And I said, I have looked, and behold a candlestick all of gold, with a bowl upon the top of it, and his seven lamps thereon, and seven pipes to the seven lamps, which are upon the top thereof: And two olive trees by it, one upon the right side of the bowl, and the other upon the left side thereof. So I answered and spake to the angel that talked with me, saying, What are these, my lord? Then the angel that talked with me answered and said unto me, Knowest thou not what these be? And I said, No, my lord. Then he answered and spake unto me, saying, This is the word of the LORD unto Zerubbabel, saying, Not by might, nor by power, but by my spirit, saith the LORD of hosts"*
*(Zechariah 4:6).*

As we pursue life's goals, we can be assured of success when the Lord is with us and when his operative power is at work for us. This is even more so when we are embarking on some mission that the Lord has commissioned us to. We are only assured of success when his operative power –the power of the

49

Holy Ghost -- is at work and is in play in our situation and circumstances.

In other words, especially for the things the Lord himself tells us, initiates, and informs us about, we are only assured of success in achieving our goals and aspirations when we are in a position of surrender and submission to the way and the play of his Spirit. This is easy enough to state, but not as easy to do. Being accustomed to move out of the way and give God room to operate, lead and direct us by his Spirit is something we typically must learn, many times through difficulties and even failure. But nonetheless, if we are to be successful in achieving the end of our expectations, particularly those things the Lord has spoken to us about we need to learn and understand the mechanisms of moving out of the way and allowing God to move in with his way and his play.

In our main Scripture text above, the angel comes to Zechariah with the intent of showing him a new vision, a new prospect. He shakes Zechariah out of his lethargy and says to him: *"What seest thou?"* We are then told that Zechariah "looked", as in he 'saw' or began to see the vision of God unfold before him. Zechariah can describe what he sees to the angel.

Many times, we are shown something by the Lord after we are similarly shaken or stirred out of our spiritual lethargy and we can describe, sometimes happily, what we are shown by the Lord. This is generally a good feeling, because we can "see" a new path or prospect the Lord has in store.

However, many times too this exhilaration is short-lived, as we are suddenly struck with the realization that great as the vision is we really have no real clue about its actual meaning —or if we do, we have no reckoning of how it could be possible; we are bemused somewhat as we ponder its plausibility and possibility.

Zechariah was no different. After seeing the vision, he was struck with bemusement as to its meaning, and he asked: *"What are these, my lord?"* In John 3:1-9 Nicodemus had a similar experience after our Lord revealed to him some great spiritual truths, and he similarly asks the Lord: *"How can these things be?"*

Invariably, after seeing the vision, if truly this is a vision from God, we still require the Lord to revisit us at some point along the path to realization and help us to properly understand and become adjusted to the true meaning, the true import, and the essential ingredient in what He had shown in the original vision – in order for us to make meaningful progress in bringing it to pass; in bringing about the desired outcomes. This can never be a journey in which the flesh can achieve real traction. It can only be by the Spirit of the Lord. Apostle Paul himself once said that having begun in the Spirit, we cannot be made perfect by the flesh (Galatians 3:3). Every true vision will begin in the Spirit and be ripened and perfected in the Spirit, and not the flesh.

What followed in reply to Zachariah's question is true of every aspiration and desire that emanates from a vision or directive from God: *"This is the word of the LORD unto Zerubbabel, saying, Not by might, nor by power, but by my spirit, saith the LORD of hosts."*

Again, the only way we will achieve our desired objectives and goals – objectives and goals set for us by the Lord – is by the Spirit of the Lord. This is a very searching statement, but one we must consider and contemplate very seriously.

Zerubbabel knew the will of the Lord but didn't yet know the Lord's way. Joshua knew the Lord's will regarding Israel's conquest of Canaan but didn't know the Lord's way. And so, Joshua walked around all night outside Jericho's walls, until he came upon the angel standing sentry. Joshua would say to him: *"Are you for us or for our enemies?"* To which the angel replied: *"Neither. But as Captain of the Lord's armies am I now come."* The angel represented the Lord's way and the Lord's play; he wasn't coming to be measured by or made subservient to Joshua's way.

The angel represented the Spirit of the Lord and his plans to bring about the salvation that Israel desired in accordance with the purposes of God. He proceeded to take over and assume control of the campaign with the command to Joshua: *"And the captain of the LORD'S host said unto Joshua, Loose thy shoe from off thy foot; for the place whereon thou standest is holy. And Joshua did so"* (Joshua 5:13-15).

If we are going to bring about the vision that the Lord has purposed and proclaimed, we are going to have to come to the practical place (and this is a very practical point in our experience) where we "loose the shoes from off our feet", because the place upon which we desire to tread, the path we desire to follow, is holy.

**WALKING UPON HOLY GROUND**

As the priests in the ancient tabernacle of Moses, and similarly in the Temple of Solomon, progressed through the sanctuary from the outer Gate or entrance through the Vail and into the Holiest, the space or enclosure in which they moved became smaller and smaller. As we move further into God's presence in terms of our fellowship, communion, and inter-relationship with him we are going to find (much to our initial consternation) that we have less and less room to do our own thing and utilize our own methods other than the methods and directives of God. And where and when God is not yet giving direction, we will not be able to do much more than wait —until the Lord again begins to move and give direction. This is the paradigm and pattern by which God does his wonders. We will learn to subdue and bring under subjection the flesh, specifically the will of the flesh. In its place we will learn to abide in and surrender to the promptings and leanings of the Spirit of God —to bring about God's outcomes; outcomes that are miraculous; outcomes that are dynamic and supernatural.

*"This I say then, Walk in the Spirit, and ye shall not fulfil the lust of the flesh. For the flesh lusteth against the Spirit, and the Spirit against the flesh: and these are contrary the one to the other: so that ye cannot do the things that ye would. But if ye be led of the Spirit, ye are not under the law. Now the works of the flesh are manifest, which are these; Adultery, fornication, uncleanness, lasciviousness, Idolatry, witchcraft, hatred, variance, emulations, wrath, strife, seditions, heresies, Envyings, murders, drunkenness, revellings, and such like: of the which I tell you before, as I have also told you in time past, that they which do such things shall not inherit the kingdom of God. But the fruit of*

the Spirit is love, joy, peace, longsuffering, gentleness, goodness, faith, Meekness, temperance: against such there is no law. And they that are Christ's have crucified the flesh with the affections and lusts. If we live in the Spirit, let us also walk in the Spirit. Let us not be desirous of vain glory, provoking one another, envying one another" (Galatians 5:16-26).

We are not going to achieve Divine outcomes while utilizing earthly or carnal methods –no matter how noble, valiant, or praiseworthy. We will only achieve the outcomes that compare to the standards set in the original vision God gave us when we employ the way and the play of the Holy Ghost. Only by the Spirit of the Lord might we achieve God's standard of spiritual outcomes for our lives. This is not easy but is something we learn by experience and typically through a period of travail and, occasionally, failures.

Moses learnt this the hard way, too. He tried early in his life to bring about God's outcomes for Israel through nobility and bravery –he meted out summary justice by slaying an Egyptian tormentor and freeing an Israelite slave from abuse. Unfortunately, this brought about the opposite outcome to what Moses anticipated. He fled Egypt –he who was considered an heir to the throne –and became an exile.

Forty years passed without event –all because Moses was not operating by the power of the Spirit but by the force of good and noble intentions. By the time God was ready for Moses, Moses was no longer ready for God –the old Moses wasn't. But there was a newer Moses now –one that the old Moses didn't know existed. This new Moses was bereft of delusions of self-worth or the worth of his own ideas and methods. This new Moses was docile and one that God could use and work with. This new Moses didn't have a will that readily collided with the will of God. As a result, the Spirit of God used Moses to bring about the outcomes that God desired for him and for the people of Israel.

Whatever you are believing God for, whatever you are standing in faith for, whatever your spiritual struggles --you will only get real traction in your journey and in the outplay of God's hand when you learn how to get in lockstep with the Spirit of God. When you learn God's way and God's play. In fact, you may never learn God's way. But learn how to get out of the way and let God lead. Let God commandeer your journey: let the Spirit of God do his work. Let God bring about Divine outcomes, miraculous outcomes, by his Spirit.

The Grace of the Lord Jesus Christ be with you.

# CHAPTER EIGHT
# EMPOWERED

*"I have set the LORD always before me: because he is at my right hand, I shall not be moved. Therefore my heart is glad, and my glory rejoiceth: my flesh also shall rest in hope. For thou wilt not leave my soul in hell; neither wilt thou suffer thine Holy One to see corruption. Thou wilt shew me the path of life: in thy presence is fulness of joy; at thy right hand there are pleasures for evermore." (Psalm 16:8-11)*

Recently, I entered a period of great stress and pressures that tested me sore and stretched me thin. I began to talk to the Lord and express my acute discontent. I prayed and communed with the Lord daily and pressed him about my situation and the dissatisfaction that I felt. I challenged him concerning my circumstances.

On this particular night, I was very perplexed and I went to bed with a questioning mind, asking the Lord, "Why?" As soon as I drifted off to sleep I entered the dream state and began to see visions of God.

**THE FIRST VISION**

I was driving a car along the road. I passed through a tollway and suddenly, I was caught by a tollway alarm of the sort that signals a violation or infraction and I was made to pull over. I checked myself in the vehicle to make sure my seat belt was secure and everything else was in order. I decided to reverse my car out of the tollway and re-enter from a different direction in the hope that I could beat the alarm and not get caught.

When I re-entered the tollway from a different direction, I was again caught by the alarm and signaled to pull over. Not wanting to pull over on the side of the ramp, I again reversed my car and made to re-enter from yet another direction --in the hope that I could beat the alarm. But again, I was caught and so I decided to pull over and wait for what comes next.

What came next was that I heard an advisory over the PA system that anybody caught on the ramp and forced to pull over must be airlifted off the ramp into the sky. Still trying to come to terms with what that meant, I began to see (from within my vehicle where I was still seated) from up above a huge airship or air- chariot of some sort descending from the sky. I was then made to understand that when the airship makes its descent to a certain level above my vehicle, it would deploy and attach itself to my vehicle and lift me into the skies.

When I realized that this was what was coming next, I began to panic. I became very anxious and disturbed about the prospect of being "airlifted" in my vehicle to some unknown destination high in the skies above. I imagined how I would feel and how I would endure the experience --how I might react -- while ascending through the heavens as I am carried in this chariot and leaving the familiarity of the solid earth beneath me. And then I awoke.

I rose from my bed and went to use the restroom. When I returned, I sat down and meditated on the vision. I knew it wasn't a sign of my passing because my time is not up... I haven't finished my work on earth. I recalled that in the Bible chariots have been used to visit prophets and sometimes convey them to Heaven. Elijah was carried by a fiery chariot and translated to Heaven. So, I said: "Maybe the Lord wants to talk to me or something" --since the voice in the vision had said: "whoever is caught by this alarm must be carried up into the skies." So, I said: "So be it." And I went back to bed. Again, I passed straight into the dream state.

## THE SECOND VISION

I saw myself in the spacious office of a CEO-type individual and as I looked across the bureau/desk the CEO seated behind it was the Lord himself. There were other people coming and going, needing help of one sort or the other, and the Lord was helping them. I saw others that came in who were not supposed to have access to that office, and they were forcibly removed.

The Lord talked and held conversation with me, and I became very comfortable in his company. After a while, it seemed like there was some kind of emergency that required his attention --and the Lord left with his entourage.

As I awaited his return, it dawned on me that I had become so comfortable in his presence that I hadn't addressed the reason for my being there. So, I resolved that upon the Lord's return I would ensure that I move to address that matter quickly lest I miss the opportunity, since I don't know when I will have the opportunity again.

The Lord returned with his entourage and immediately became absorbed once again in helping people who were around him when I seized my opportunity: I measured myself and politely addressed myself to him and said: "Lord, please, I wanted to let you know that you still haven't settled me... I'm still not settled as far as my aspirations and my expectations --you haven't settled me yet..."

The Lord looked at me with so much empathy and sympathy --reaching out to me --and said: "I know... I know... I haven't forgotten you... I haven't forgotten..." He kept saying that and he held me... When He did that, I said to him: "You know I believe in you... You know I really believe in you". And the Lord said: "I know... I know..."

And then I woke up.

I have been so empowered by this extraordinary experience. I said to myself: "So this is why the Lord called for me... This is what He wanted to show me." He wanted to reassure me of his love and goodwill toward me. He wanted to re-invigorate me. He wanted to re-energize me and give me renewed hope concerning his plans for me, concerning his agenda for me.

I continued to meditate on the things I had seen and heard and thought about how I could also extract something from that experience that I could use as a basis for delivering instruction and direction for the Church, for my sermon the next Sunday. I picked up my Bible and at random it opened to Jeremiah 29:11-13. As I looked at the scripture verses clueless as to what they meant for me right that moment --or how they tied into what I had experienced --all of a sudden, they unraveled before me like a flower, and I understood what the Lord was saying in those verses and how they correlated with the visions I had experienced. I now knew the presentation and instruction to give to the Church.

## JEREMIAH 29:11-13

*"For I know the thoughts that I think toward you, saith the Lord, thoughts of peace, and not of evil, to give you an expected end. Then shall ye call upon me, and ye shall go and pray unto me, and I will hearken unto you. And ye shall seek me, and find me, when ye shall search for me with all your heart."*

First and foremost, we can be rest assured that the Lord's thoughts toward us are thoughts of peace, thoughts of comfort, and thoughts of consolation. Those are the Lord's primary thoughts toward us. If you are struggling to make ends meet, then be rest assured that those are not the Lord's thoughts concerning you. If you are wrestling with illness, then be rest assured that those are not the Lord's thoughts concerning you. If you are broken and bowed by the weight of life's problems, pressures and strains then be rest assured in the knowledge that those are not the Lord's thoughts concerning you. Rather, those are altogether the thoughts of Satan, whom our Lord has told us:

*"cometh not but to steal, to kill, and to destroy."* Whereas Jesus came, by his own declaration, *"that you may have life, and have it more abundantly."* So, in the very first instance, when we are tried, tested, and tempered -- broken, bowed, and beaten --we should realize that THE LORD'S THOUGHTS TOWARD US ARE THOUGHTS OF PEACE, NOT OF EVIL; TO BRING US TO AN EXPECTED END, TO AN EXPECTATION, TO A FUTURE AND A HOPE.

However, there are three principles the Lord wants us to be mindful of to ensure that we can fully reap the benefits of his goodwill toward us and his good thoughts toward us --and He speaks to these principles in the verses from that Scripture in Jeremiah referenced above.

## YE SHALL CALL UPON ME, AND YE SHALL GO

As I said before, when I initially opened these verses at random, I stared at them thinking to myself: "Okay, so how does all this correlate with what happened to me? What does all this mean for the Church and my Sunday sermon?" And then the Lord opened my eyes to see what He was saying in those verses.

The first thing the Lord wants us to be mindful of to reap the benefits of his goodwill is that we must learn to call upon him before we go: *"Then ye shall call upon me, and ye shall go...".* Before we embark on any journey, before we begin any series of plans, before we adopt any new business or other social contract --we must first call upon the Lord. We must acknowledge him and his primacy in all our ways and paths, so that He may give us direction.

*"Commit thy way unto the Lord; trust also in him; and he*

*shall bring it to pass." (Psalm 37:5)*

*"In all thy ways acknowledge him, and he shall direct thy paths." (Proverbs 3:6)*

Sometimes, and for some of us, we are not at that point where we confidently can ask the Lord for a definitive answer as to "Yes" or "No" regarding a proposed or intended route or course of action. But we can always commit our proposed journey to the Lord nonetheless, and trust that if it is his will, He will bring it to pass. And if it is not, He will bring it to a halt before we suffer any damage or hurt.

Even when we are confident that the path or course we are taking is the will of the Lord, we should still commit it to him before we begin the journey. So that He will show and guide us along his way, notwithstanding the fact we have correctly understood his will. Remember that our Lord in the Garden of Gethsemane prayed: *"Father, if it is possible let this cup pass from me; Nevertheless, not my will but thine be done...".* As I said earlier, depending on the extreme circumstances, stress, and emotion of the moment it is not always practical for us to expect to hear a clear and definitive Word from God regarding a prospective path. So, in those types of situations we should pray according to the example of our Lord when he expressed himself thus: *"Father, if it is possible let this cup pass from me;' Nevertheless, not my will but thine be done...".* In the knowledge and trust that God, knowing our hearts, will direct our steps to fall in tandem and in sync with his perfect will in that situation --no matter how unclear that express will might be to us. *"Ye shall call upon me, and ye shall*

*go".* Or, before you 'Go' you must first 'Call upon Me'... That is the first principle.

## AND PRAY UNTO ME, AND I WILL HEARKEN UNTO YOU

The second thing is that we must, each of us individually, learn how to pray and get an answer from Heaven. We must learn to pray to God such that He will hearken to us. That is the kind of prayer we must learn to pray. We must unlearn the method of praying for praying sake; or praying for the sake of having prayed --or praying for the sake of being noted as having prayed. Hear what our Lord says about these kinds of prayer:

*"And when thou prayest, thou shalt not be as the hypocrites are: for they love to pray standing in the synagogues and in the corners of the streets, that they may be seen of men. Verily I say unto you, They have their reward." (Matthew 6:5)*

This kind of prayer and any modeled after it will not yield practical results, although it might comfort the mind of the one who has thus prayed (and those around him) in the belief that they have "prayed" things through. This kind of prayer will not produce results, because --as our Lord pointed out --the one who has thus prayed has already received his reward: i.e., the 'answer' to his 'prayer'. The answer being the open recognition, attention, and mental pacifier this prayer brings. And that is the only 'reward' that this kind of prayer will get.

We must never pray for the sake of praying. Rather when we pray, we should do so because --and only because --we expect an answer from God. We expect to have a conversation with God. We expect God to respond to us in some way or

63

fashion. Let me say this again: the kind of prayer the children of God should be praying is the kind of prayer that puts God on the spot, as it were. We must have prayer thresholds, whereby we hold God to account, and we can measure ourselves and our progress in ascending the ladder of grace by keeping track and watching to see what God will do in response.

## HABAKUKK SAYS:

*"I will stand upon my watch, and set me upon the tower, and will watch to see what He will say unto me, and what I shall answer when I am reproved." (Habakukk 2:1)*

The prophets and saints of old were men and women who prayed with the purport of getting a response from God --and watching to see what, when, where, and how the Lord would answer back. Too many of us pray and then walk away and think nothing else of it. Or we pray then remain pacified and comforted in the thought that we have offered our prayers --and that's that. Not so. The writer of the Book of Hebrews admonishes us that: *"...Without faith it is impossible to please him: for He that cometh to God must believe that he is, and that he is a rewarder of them that diligently seek him." (Hebrews 11:6)*

When we come to God, when we come to prayer, we must do so in the belief --and we must have the attitude --that God is going to respond to us somehow and some way and press him to do so --*"He is a rewarder of them that diligently seek him."*

This is the second principle the Lord sought to impress upon his people; *"...And ye shall pray, and I will hearken unto you";* i.e., learn how to pray and get Heaven's attention. Learn how

to pray and get an answer.

## AND YE SHALL SEEK ME, AND FIND ME...

The third principle is that when we set out to seek God, we should be sure that it is God we find --and not something else: *"Ye shall seek Me, and find Me..."*

Too often, when we seek God for something and along the way something else is presented to us our attention is easily diverted and we are derailed from our path --so that in the end we fall short of or otherwise complicate the promise of God. Too many of us have developed spiritual ADD (attention deficit disorder) and are incapable of maintaining focus on the things of God. We start something but can't finish it. We embark on a journey but become distracted and abandon it when something else that appears deceptively worthwhile presents itself. We cannot wait for God to show up, and so we do not find God in the end.

In the Old Testament, we read the story of how King Saul was given a commission to destroy Amalek, the enemies of God, without fear or favor and to spare none. However, when Saul took Amalek, he became deceived by the good things he saw in the camp of Amalek and reserved the choice spoil for himself and his company. Saul also spared Agag the King of Amalek, being impressed with Agag against the Lord's express wishes. As a result, Saul did not find favor with God. But what he found for himself (the spoils of Amalek) proved his undoing.

When Samuel appeared, Saul was rebuked and the kingdom was torn from him (see 1 Samuel 15:1-35*): "And ye shall* *seek me, and find me"* (and only me, says the Lord). When we set out to do God's will, we must ensure that it is God that we find at the end --and not something else. Another way of saying this is that it is not enough to be called by God, but we must also ensure that we do God's will (through and through). Too many people are called of God to a particular vocation (i.e., ministers, public servants, teachers, etc.) but many of them do not do God's will when they enter the office. Or if they start out doing God's will, they eventually become diverted, distracted, or enticed by other things besides God (mostly opportunity, license, benefits etc.) and end up doing their own version of God's will --albeit under the banner of the original vocation they received from God. Hear the Lord again: *"And ye shall seek Me, and ye shall find Me".*

The key to being successful in seeking God is to be sure to keep your heart singly for God, to be focused on him and none other. He said: *"And ye shall seek me, and find me, when ye shall search for me with all your heart";* i.e., when you search for me and only me... When you are serious about finding me, and me only. Sometimes this singleness of heart only becomes possible through travail, through failure, and learning the hard lessons that experience teaches the uninitiated. It is then that we are mellow and develop the sharpness and keenness of spirit to be attentive to the Lord and wait for him for as long as He will take to show up in our situation. When we set out to seek him, we must be sure that it is him that we find --and none other.

These are the three principles that the Lord enjoined me to share with his people, to exhort them to be strong in the faith and seek him without ceasing and without fail. His thoughts towards them are thoughts of peace, and not of evil; to bring them to a safe and prosperous harbor: to give them a future and a hope. It is the Lord's will that his people should be at peace, in safety, and prosper in all things.

These are some of the things that will serve to empower the saints, to educate them, retool them to be able to apprehend and reap the benefits of all his goodwill toward his people. He has not forgotten you. He has not forgotten his promises toward you. He is still mindful of all his goodwill toward you. He seeks to bring you into an elevated position from where it will be easier for you to see and apprehend the blessings He has kept for you, on the one hand -- and on the other, it will be easier for him to shower the blessings on you without let or hindrance.

Continue to hold onto him. Continue to increase in faith and in the power and presence of the Lord in your life, so that there will be no hindrances to you being able to apprehend all the glories of Christ.

The Grace of our Lord Jesus Christ be with you.

# CHAPTER NINE
# THE SPOKEN WORD: THE KEY TO RECOVERING OUR DESTINY

It all began with one word.

And then a series of words.

And then another. And another after that.

And with each separate and distinct word and series of words a particular thing was done, and some other creation established here and something different over there. And then the streaming words became like a beautiful symphony, cascading with rhythm and partitioned into cadence by cadence of pulsating life in all its various forms at every level of creation.

The Gospel of John 1:1-3 puts it this way:

*"In the beginning was the Word, and the Word was with God, and the Word was God. The same was in the beginning with*

*God. All things were made by him; and without him was not anything made that was made."*

Psalm 33:9 also tells us:

*"For he spake, and it was done; he commanded, and it stood fast."*

We also understand from Isaiah 55:11 that God's word is an inviolable act or force of nature; a vibration or pulse of living energy, of life itself.

*"So shall my word be that goeth forth out of my mouth: it shall not return unto me void, but it shall accomplish that which I please, and it shall prosper in the thing whereto I sent it."*

And so basically, everything in the created universe, when resolved into its most germane, granular definition is a word that was spoken; a pulse or a vibration from God, and the stream of words or vibrations produced by him created a rhythmic cadence that defined every life-form and the levels of life at which they exist.

We are told in Hebrews 1:1-3 that the Son, who is the Word of God, is the lifeblood or pulse that describes the base atomic construct of all things, including the angelic universe.

*"God, who at sundry times and in divers manners spake in time past unto the fathers by the prophets, Hath in these last days spoken unto us by his Son, whom he hath appointed heir of all things, by whom also he made the worlds; Who being the brightness of his glory, and the express image of his person, and*

*upholding all things by the word of his power, when he had by himself purged our sins, sat down on the right hand of the Majesty on high; Being made so much better than the angels, as he hath by inheritance obtained a more excellent name than they."*

Everything in this universe when resolved into its most basic, simple form is a word, a pulse, or a vibration. Creatures are differentiated on different levels of power and strength on this basis of vibrations at the atomic level. At the lowest level is the physical creation where vibrations are at their slowest rhythm. The spectrum in which humans can see light is very limited, and the frequency at which we can hear sound unaided is very base. There are some higher frequencies of sound that are not audible to the human ear but are audible to other creatures like dogs and cats, for instance. And this is the principle used in dog whistles that produce sounds which you or I cannot hear but a dog can hear.

When we move into a higher cadence of rhythmic vibration that defines creation at a higher level, i.e., the spiritual world, we find that there are many more colors that exist in creation but which the human eye, the natural eye, cannot see. There are also rhythms and sounds which one can hear in Heaven that would be impossible to translate or reproduce in the natural. Again, because these belong to a higher cadence of life; one that is pulsating at a much more rapid rate than our natural human senses can detect.

We also find that in the heavenly places, spirits are defined and limited by the specific cadence in which they can naturally exist and function. And so on and so forth, until we come to God himself. God dwells in the highest Heaven that there is, and the Glory of this realm and the cadence of its rhythmic harmony is so elevated that every other thing, person, and process in the created universe may as well be standing still (i.e., in relation to the elevated frequencies, rhythmic vibrations and movements that play host to God's presence and our incapacity to effectively detect them unaided by the Spirit of God). God dwells in such an elevated position of Glory that He can stand in one spot and from there glance backward at 'events' or observe them as they might exist presently; or, further still, glance forward at the same events to see how they might appear in what we would call the future –and all in a swift moment.

Because of this Divine property, our Lord describes himself this way in Revelation 8:

*"I am Alpha and Omega, the beginning and the ending, saith the Lord, which is, and which was, and which is to come, the Almighty."*

That is to say, God can observe or stand in all places past, present, and future --or from beginning through to the end --at the same time. That is his property as God.

Romans 4:17 similarly says of him:

*"God, who quickeneth the dead, and calleth those things which be not as though they were."*

In any effort to build a structure or edifice the first and foremost thing is to lay a proper foundation. A building or structure may exude elegance and architectural brilliance, but if its foundation is not properly laid or of the correct material the building will fail, and its faulty construction will lead to eventual collapse. The foundation is of paramount importance in any construct.

Following this pattern, The Lord laid a proper foundation of pristine quality –His Word. *"In the beginning was the Word, and the Word was with GOD and the Word was GOD..."*

In several Scriptures, we are made to understand that GOD conceived his thoughts about you and me (His creation) before the foundation of the world (Ephesians 1:4; Hebrews 4:3; Matthew 13:35; 1 Peter 1:20; Revelation 13:8).

Having then defined us in His divine thought and intention, His "Word", He spoke that word concerning you and me into existence:

*"All things were made by him; and without him was not anything (or anyone) made that was made."*

Therefore, your life, your existence and everything about it was pre-conceived by GOD in his thought and purpose; purpose which was then unfolded by the SPOKEN WORD in the form of your spiritual and physical materialization in this hour and moment in time. It stands to reason that when our lives appear to be in a state of disarray and confusion –when we find ourselves in a state of disrepair due to trials and troubles, etc. –there must be something that has impacted against us and caused us to veer off course out of our original, predetermined orbit and path. Agents of darkness, those manifold and varied adversarial elemental forces are culprits here whose mission is to alter our destiny and derail and destroy the plan, purpose, and prescription of the Lord in our lives —a prescription of good and not of evil.

What is the remedy to these things? In Matthew 6:10 our Lord taught us to SPEAK our deliverance and realignment with GOD's original Word, design, and destiny for us with the words: *"Thy kingdom come. Thy will* (i.e., your original Word defining our destiny) *be done in earth* (i.e., be fully recovered and realized in our lives), *as it is in heaven* (i.e., according to the o r i g i n a l imprint and copy of this Will and Word in the heavenly archive).

We must learn to SPEAK the Word —GOD's Word concerning us —into existence and thereby recover that which is lost to Satan and his hosts. We must learn to recover the original foundation that was laid in this universe governing our existence — the Word that GOD spoke, defined, and described concerning you and I before the foundation of the world.

That's what we ought to do as Christians. We ought to learn to speak the words that GOD has spoken concerning us.

# CHAPTER TEN
# LET GOD BE TRUE, BUT EVERY MAN A LIAR

*"For what if some did not believe? shall their*
*unbelief make the faith of God without effect?*
*God forbid: yea, let God be true, but every man a liar; as it is written,*
*That thou mightest be justified in thy sayings, and mightest*
*overcome when thou art judged." (Romans 3:3-4)*

Is it possible to invalidate God's word or void God's purpose? There are too many instances in contemporary society and in the public space where the conventional wisdom based on current norms and practices would appear to have voided and rendered obsolete the clear, concise, and express declarations of God on an issue. We do not need to elaborate here but the evidence of this is abundantly obvious for all to see.

It appears that there are some express declarations of God in the Scriptures which many in the Churches particularly have taken liberty to vary and re-interpret to align with contemporary thinking and social custom –thereby presuming to invalidate God's own word. And things appear to go on without incident or challenge from Above –for the present, at least. And so, many assume that, perhaps, God has allowed change or reinterpretation of his word in line with what is convenient and contemporary for the times.

So, again, is it possible to invalidate God's express instructions? Does God himself accept a situation where we presume or purport to invalidate his express and declarative wisdom as enunciated in his word, whether spoken or written?

This is a rhetorical question that Apostle Paul put to the Romans in his epistle, with specific regard to the Jews' failure to attain righteousness and salvation through the observance of the Law. Did their failure invalidate God's word? The answer is no. Regardless of what men do (or don't) God's word is sacred and remains so. At the end, as the Scriptures say in Romans 3:3-4 and Psalm 51:4 respectively, God's word will validate itself – because it will still hold true, and offenders will be held to account. They will be judged. Ultimately, when we fail to uphold God's originally defined mandates the failure will be ours and though for the present it may appear like He has allowed us to have our way, we will account for it in the end. We will be held to the correct standard in the end. God will not allow us to obviate his own standard due to personal inconvenience.

*"For what if some did not believe? shall their unbelief make the faith of God without effect? God forbid: yea, let God be true, but every man a liar; as it is written, That thou mightest be justified in thy sayings, and mightest overcome when thou art*

*judged." (Romans 3:3-4)*

*"Against thee, thee only, have I sinned, and done this evil in thy sight: that thou mightest be justified when thou speakest, and be clear when thou judgest." (Psalm 51:4)*

## WHAT IS YOUR FAITH WORTH?

The question this brings up is this: what is the price of your faith? What is the price of your vision? The vision that God gave you. The mandate that God gave you. Why did Judas betray Jesus Christ? Did Judas hate the Lord? Probably not. So, why did he betray him? Judas betrayed the Lord Jesus Christ (the manifested Word of God) because the path the Lord was taking – i.e., a path of direct conflict with the established religious order and system of the day –did not offer a desirable endgame for Judas. Like many of us, Judas was happy to serve the Lord and hope to cash-out someday, i.e., to hope to have a big payday and something for posterity. But the path the Lord was taking didn't have a desirable endgame in view –at least not to Judas' eye. It didn't have a desirable endgame for Peter and the others, either. Which is why Peter tried to dissuade our Lord from taking what Peter considered an unconciliatory path to conflict with the establishment and the Lord rebuked him with the words: *"Get behind me Satan."* However, Peter's reservations about the Lord's chosen path didn't go as far as Judas'.

In the end, Judas was prepared to sell the 'vision', the Word that God gave in the person of Jesus Christ, for money. His faith had a price. His vision had a price. The price was thirty pieces of silver. It is possible that Judas erroneously calculated that the

Lord would use his power to evade capture as He had done on other occasions (see John 8:58; Luke 4:28-30; John 5:13) – thereby ensuring Judas would get his money without having blood on his hands. That would explain why when it became clear that the Lord was not going to resist his arrest and the consequences, Judas hastened back in desperation to his paymasters to return the money, which they refused. At that point, we are told Judas cast the blood money on the floor and went out to hang himself. Judas' faith, his vision, and the mandates he received from God had a price.

For many men and women of God, God gave them a mandate, a vision, a commission when they began which in due course, they had cause to vary. They had cause to change. They had cause to dilute. All because their faith had a price, and they gave in to the desires of flesh, the expectations of man. They gave in to the standards, metrics, and indices that others placed upon them and began to measure themselves by a different measure besides the measure of God. To please the people. To please family. To please friends or to please themselves –they sold their vision, their mandate for earthly satisfaction or rewards. For the approval of men. For the accreditation and acceptance of certain groups. For convenience they sold the vision and think that God's apparent silence is tantamount to acquiescence. They assume his silence is passive approval. No, it is not.

**THE COST OF YOUR VISION**

Every vision or mandate has a cost associated with it. This could be something that the Lord tells you about up front like He did when He said to Ananias concerning Paul in Acts 9:15-16:

*"But the Lord said unto him, Go thy way: for he is a chosen vessel unto me, to bear my name before the Gentiles, and kings, and the children of Israel: for I will shew him HOW GREAT THINGS HE MUST SUFFER FOR MY NAME'S SAKE."*

Or it is something you discover when you begin to walk the vision day-by-day. Either way, you only really come to grips with the cost as you walk in it daily. And then it becomes a part of your experience and the stark reality hits you about what exactly this vision will cost you personally.

Sometimes, the cost is to the ministry or to the church --for pastors and ministers. What do you do when the path the Lord is leading you, in the first instance, appears to run contrary to your perceived interests or those of your Church or Ministry? Can the expectations of others, people who have legitimate reason to have expectations of you (like your church, your peers or your family), trump the word of God, i.e. the vision, the mandates, the commission the Lord gave you originally? Can those considerations invalidate God's original word to you?

I ask again the question of what do you do when the path the Lord is leading on runs contrary to your own perceived interests and your understanding of the ministry?

Abraham was given a mandate from the Lord that was symbolized in Isaac, the child of promise. Isaac would be the forbear or procreator to a chosen generation of blessed people of God. Turn to the next page of Abraham's story and the same God is telling Abraham to take the same Isaac and offer him up as a sacrifice? Doesn't that appear to run contrary to the vision and mandate God originally gave Abraham? Make no mistake, this was no easy choice for Abraham. We don't know how long it took him to make up his mind, but he ultimately decided, just like Apostle Paul did, to "Let God be true, and every [consideration, expectation, desire, and vested interest of] man be a liar." He was not going to vary the word of God because it appeared to be in acute conflict with his personal interests or in conflict with the work of God through the chosen seed, Isaac. Abraham resolved that he would obey God rather than man (i.e., the emotions of man, the rational thinking of man, the desires of man or the interests of man) believing that as long as he obeyed God it would be up to God to fill in the 'gaps' of his guidance (i.e., to raise Isaac from the dead if it became necessary, as Paul explains in Hebrews 11:19). Abraham did not sell or mortgage the vision for immediate personal gain or comfort, and he was rewarded for it.

We already know the story of how Esau sold and willingly forfeited his vision, his promise, for a bowl of pottage –because of acute inconvenience during a particular period of his life. When he later recovered his senses and sought to regain the vision or promise he was denied, *"though he sought it carefully with tears."* (Heb. 12:16-17).

We also see the example of King Saul in 1 Samuel 13:8-14, where Saul decided he could wait for Samuel no longer because Samuel tarried for seven days beyond the set time and *the people had begun to disperse from the camp*. So, Saul proceeded to offer the sacrifice that only Samuel ought to offer. The Lord rebuked Saul and tore the kingdom from him that day because of his disobedience. Because he elevated and regarded the expectation and desire of man above and beyond God's expressly declared mandate.

So, in our situation as pastors and ministers, how do we react or respond when despite obedience to God's word and the vision He has expressly delivered we see the church or ministry apparently waning and people beginning to disengage and depart —as was the case with Saul? What do we do? Do we act like Saul did and innovate and improvise in the attempt to 'salvage' the situation? Or do we strengthen ourselves in God and declare with Apostle Paul: "Let God be true, and every [consideration, expectation, desire, and vested interest of] man be a liar"?

God ultimately will not accept a situation where we vary his word and out of convenience bring to him, perhaps like Cain did, a more beautiful and elegant 'sacrifice' than Abel. God will not accept that sacrifice either now or at the Judgement any more than He accepted Cain's. Make no mistake: Cain knew very well what God expected of him as did Abel. We know this because God said so when He rebuked Cain: *"But unto Cain and to his offering he had not respect. And Cain was very wroth, and his countenance fell. And the LORD said unto Cain, Why art thou wroth? and why is thy countenance fallen? If thou doest well, shalt thou not be accepted?"* (Genesis 4:5-7)

So, Cain chose not to perform the express requirements of God because what he eventually did was more convenient (for Cain) —and God rejected it.

There will be a lot of disappointment and headache at the Judgement when God weighs the works of his servants, because a lot of 'beautiful' ministry work will be discarded – because it is the result of men and women of God, people that the Lord himself sent, varying, and changing their mandate out of convenience and expecting that God will still 'consider' their 'sacrifice' in his name.

## A RECKONING EVEN NOW

Even presently, God is acting against men and women of God who despite apparent success and acclaim do not obey him. Do not obey his word. Do not obey his mandates. They take God's word as something that can be varied, something that can be changed out of convenience, to satisfy an apparent need, to meet a more pressing and rewarding standard, to prevent collapse of a circle of trust or of friends —or whatever rational thought, excuse or pretext that can be conjured to excuse willful disobedience to and variance from either God's written word or his expressly declared divine mandates.

God's word must be obeyed. God must be glorified and reverenced by obedience to his word, by obedience to his vision, to his mandates —when it is convenient and when it is inconvenient.

Let God be true, and every man be a liar. Let friends fail – but let God be true and we true to his word. Let opportunities fail

– but let God be true and we true to his word. Let peers fail --but let God be true and we true to his word. Let the very thing that God established itself appear to fail --but let God be true and we true to his word. Let God fill in the blanks. Let him resolve himself within his own declarative word.

We really cannot afford to lose the vision or the mandates the Lord has given to us. The Lord will require of us an accounting. Things will have to add up on his ledger not just on ours. Unfortunately, a lot of folks generally discover this fact a little too late for their own good.

The grace of our Lord Jesus Christ be with you.

## CHAPTER ELEVEN
# GOD IS HIS OWN INTERPRETER

*"Now when John had heard in the prison the works of Christ, he sent two of his disciples, And said unto him, Art thou he that should come, or do we look for another? Jesus answered and said unto them, Go and shew John again those things which ye do hear and see: The blind receive their sight, and the lame walk, the lepers are cleansed, and the deaf hear, the dead are raised up, and the poor have the gospel preached to them. And blessed is he, whosoever shall not be offended in me."*
*(Matthew 11:2-6)*

God cannot exist in a vacuum. His nature is such that He cannot be limited or contained. Nor can the discovery of him be exhausted, exhaustively mapped or navigated. His is not a nature that can be completely defined in scope or whose boundaries can be delineated. God is boundless.

In the book of Isaiah 66:1, He declares:

*"The heaven is my throne, and the earth is my footstool: where is the house that ye build unto me? And where is the place of my rest?"*

In accordance with this truth, we are told by the Apostle in John 21:25:

*"And there are also many other things which Jesus did, the which, if they should be written every one, I suppose that even the world itself could not contain the books that should be written. Amen."*

It is not possible to clearly demarcate or describe God in scope, in measure and in manifestations. Our Lord labored to prepare not only his disciples at the time when He walked the earth but also those who would come to worship and serve him thereafter – you and I – to receive and walk with God and His Word. To be able to understand, process, and ultimately obey His Word.

In John 16:13 our Lord taught:

*"when he, the Spirit of truth, is come, he will guide you into all truth: for he shall not speak of himself; but whatsoever he shall hear, that shall he speak: and he will shew you things to come."*

Our Lord further assured His disciples that: *"...whither I go ye know, and the way ye know.".* That is to say, *"by now you should've received my Word regarding my journey and have a better understanding of what this journey means, what it represents; what is its ultimate significance to you and to the world."*

Of course, like you and I, the disciples had received his Word and stewed over it. They had debated its meaning silently among themselves. Many or maybe most had even rejected its primary premise and told him so (remember how the Lord rebuked Peter for opposing his being resigned to conflict with the Jewish rulers that would lead to his death, etc.). The disciples did not understand Jesus' words and struggled with them –like we struggle with the things God says when He is speaking to us. When God is communicating with us.

At length, the disciples asked the crucial question, at the same time admitting they were utterly flabbergasted at the things and the approach our Lord was taking: *"Lord, we know not whither thou goest; and how can we know the way?"* i.e., we haven't the faintest clue what you're talking about, Lord. That notwithstanding, you continue to assume we should know and we must know when in fact we don't know.

**GOD IS A MANIFESTATION OF HIS OWN TRUTH**

Jesus' reply was: *"I am the way, the truth, and the life: no man cometh unto the Father, but by me. If ye had known me, ye should have known my Father also: and from henceforth ye know him, and have seen him."*

Our Lord was saying (and is saying today) that we should stop stumbling over trying to find the correct interpretation to His Word and just STAND IN THE PLACE WHERE HE IS HAPPENING to receive his Word... When God is 'HAPPENING', that is his INTERPRETATION... You want to know where I'm going and to understand the way? Then stand in the place where I have ordained that you should stand so that you will be acquainted with my manifest presence. When that presence is happening around you then that, in and of itself, is the interpretation of what I said would be: *"I am the Way, the Truth and the Life..."*

It is not about a doctrine; it is about me. It is not about a school of thought; it is about me. It is about me becoming incarnate in your time and space, me filling the conditions around you with my active and unfolding purpose that is playing out right in front of you. When this happens then you have the interpretation of my words to you.

The Bible says in John 4:24: *"God is a Spirit: and they that worship him must worship him in spirit and in truth."*

That is to say, God is a Spirit, a super-elemental force that happens, that is manifested, and that is constantly manifesting. And to keep pace with Him, to walk with Him, to "worship" Him, we must not become set in our ways. We must be prepared for the unexpected. We must be prepared for the uncommon. We must be prepared for the unnatural. We must be prepared for the unnerving, i.e., we must always every time be prepared for manifestation to have the last word, to have the last say and to authenticate God's declared will. God will certify what He meant to say when He said by what He does when He brings it to pass. At that point, all the arguments can go out the window, because God has given his own interpretation to his words.

## A PLACE OF STUMBLING

This is where we stumble. This is where we founder. God appeared in accordance with His word through the prophets. He manifested himself in the person of our Lord Jesus Christ. He himself said in Matt. 5:17: *"Think not that I am come to destroy the law, or the prophets: I am not come to destroy, but to fulfil."* Also, in John 5:46: *"had ye believed Moses, ye would have believed me: for he wrote of me..."*

I don't believe Moses ever mentioned our Lord by name. Nonetheless, Moses "wrote of" him. The prophets wrote about the Lord and what He would do. The religious leaders of the day spent a good deal of time studying the Scriptures to acquaint themselves with what God had said He would do.

However, they didn't have the correct interpretation of those things, because when God himself began to interpret the words He had before spoken to the prophets – by manifesting and happening in their midst through the person of Jesus Christ -- the same Jewish leaders criticized and fought against it until our Lord rebuked them as recorded in John 5:38-40:

*"Ye have not his word abiding in you: for whom he hath sent, him ye believe not. Search the scriptures; for in them ye think ye have eternal life: and they are they which testify of me. And ye will not come to me, that ye might have life."*

Also Mark 12:24: *"And Jesus answering said unto them, Do ye not therefore err, because ye know not the scriptures, neither the power of God?"*

That is to say, even though you may 'know' the Scriptures (as with many of us) you still fall short of God's will, you fail to properly sync-up with God, you fail to recognize and align yourself with God's unfolding purpose BECAUSE YOU ARE NOT OPEN TO THE POSSIBILITIES OF GOD'S POWER OR OF WHAT

GOD CAN DO. You are not open-minded. You are closed-up as far as what you allow and disallow. Perhaps because of training, orientation, tradition, fear or just plain unbelief. You are not open to the God who exists by manifesting himself. This is the ONLY way God exists. By manifestation. By incarnation. By becoming flesh in our circumstances. By taking form and shape in our lives. So that when in fact God begins to take shape and manifest His will, when He begins to 'interpret' His own word, we should be in the position to receive Him.

**GOD HAPPENS AND GOD MANIFESTS HIS WORD**

In Luke 5:4-11, the story is told of how our Lord approached Simon Peter by the waterside and tasked him to launch out together and catch fish. Peter immediately resisted because he knew that fish do not come out to feed in the hot afternoon, they feed at night when it is cooler. Besides this, Simon protested, he had toiled all the night and had caught nothing. So, based on his prior experience, this was not a wise course of action coupled with the fact this was the wrong time of day to do it. It didn't make any sense to do what the Lord said for him to do.

And this is the challenge to us: when God begins to happen, when God begins to manifest —not our theories, not our conjectures or speculations, not even our precise expectations necessarily, but God himself; when He begins to happen in our midst --more often than not, it may come as a surprise. It may not make sense. And we tend to founder at this point. Because we usually cannot excuse or justify the risk of doing something that we can't back-up by good common sense, being the rational beings that we are.

It didn't make sense to Simon, but he decided to do it anyway – because the Lord insisted. And so, they went out into the deep.

We are going to have to trust God and just "launch out into the deep" unchartered, unfamiliar waters of God's manifestation to see Him, to achieve alignment with his purpose.

Within a short time of casting the net, suddenly it appeared like the water was coming alive somehow... There was a rippling convergence on the surface of the water around the boat they were in, and the boat experienced a 'pull' of some kind. Like something was pulling it downward. So, they jumped on it, rallied every hand on deck to try and pull the net in (now visibly weighing down the boat with fish). The net broke. So, they beckoned on a partner ship close by to come to their aid and together they struggled to eventually fill both boats with fish. Then both boats began to sink!

At this point, Simon Peter understood. Because we are told: "When Simon Peter saw it..." So, something suddenly dawned on Simon at that moment. The lights came on. He "saw" something. And what he saw scared him to the point *"he fell down at Jesus' knees, saying, Depart from me; for I am a sinful man, O Lord."* Simon now saw the Truth. And the Truth which he saw was not a doctrine, a stream of teaching or a preconception or mindset. Oh, no – all those teachings and preconceptions took to their heels, because they could stand in the presence of the

God who had just happened to Simon. God had just interpreted himself and his intentions to Simon by this manifestation to Simon. By becoming incarnate in Simon's circumstances.

## BE IN THE PLACE WHERE GOD HAPPENS

How do we properly interpret the word of God and the will of God? How do we ensure that we have the correct apprehension, comprehension and understanding of what God has spoken, of what is God's intention, of what is God's way or agenda?

In Exodus 13:19 we are told that as they made their departure out of Egyptian bondage, *"Moses took the bones of Joseph with him: for he had straitly sworn the children of Israel, saying, God will surely visit you; and ye shall carry up my bones away hence with you."*

We are again reminded in Hebrews 11:22 that *"By faith Joseph, when he died, made mention of the departing of the children of Israel; and gave commandment concerning his bones."*

Joseph gave this commandment because he knew from the Lord that the Resurrection, i.e., the manifestation of God, will happen in the holy lands and so he ensured that upon his decease his earthly remains should be transferred from the 'house of bondage' to the place where God was going to happen.

In Acts 1:4-5 our Lord charged his disciples in this manner: *"And, being assembled together with them, commanded them that they should NOT depart from Jerusalem, but wait for the promise of the Father, which, saith he, ye have heard of me.*

*For John truly baptized with water; but ye shall be baptized with the Holy Ghost not many days hence."*

The disciples tried to get into one of their analyses about how and when God should accomplish this and that. But our Lord effectively told them, "Your part is to simply obey and leave the rest to God. God is his own interpreter. When He happens, so long as you are obedient and stay in that place that He has placed or ordained for you to stay –He will happen to you and you will know."

*"When they therefore were come together, they asked of him, saying, Lord, wilt thou at this time restore again the kingdom to Israel? And he said unto them, It is not for you to know the times or the seasons, which the Father hath put in his own power. But ye shall receive power, after that the Holy Ghost is come upon you: and ye shall be witnesses unto me both in Jerusalem, and in all Judaea, and in Samaria, and unto the uttermost part of the earth."*

It could've been very difficult to abide by these instructions – after our Lord's ascension, after He departed physically from the earth. There are many reasons why the disciples would've felt compelled to stray away from that location and take care of this pressing business or that. And you can bet the devil threw all kinds of excuses and reasons at them to get them to deviate from our Lord's instructions.

But they stayed. And they stayed until God happened in their midst and in a way nothing could have prepared them for, naturally speaking. Rushing wind and tongues of fire sound pretty terrific to me. Is that something we would've willfully submitted ourselves to if it were to happen in our midst? Or would we have left the room in a hurry, prepared to watch from a safe distance while at the same time flipping the pages of our Bible to see if we can find any reference point in the scriptures to lend legitimacy to the manifestation unfolding in our midst? Or perhaps we would want to know just what accredited schools of theology Peter and the rest were associated with? Or what recognized Churches they had come out from −before we agree that this is God?

Stay in the place that God has ordained for you to be, so that you may receive the Word of God and have the grace to understand and grasp it. This will be a holy place, not a place of uncleanness.

Some of us are in the wrong relationship. God did not ordain that we should 'hook-up' with this person and that. As long as we refuse to exit that relationship, God will not happen; we will not get the interpretation of God's will.

Some of us are in the wrong company in general. As long as we do not exit this particular company of people God will not happen. We will not get the interpretation of his will.

Some of us are in the wrong Church, where we are not experiencing growth, nor are we allowed to grow. So long as we do not exit this particular group God will not happen. We will not get the interpretation of his will.

Some of us are in the wrong place vertically versus horizontally, i.e. we dwell and are fully vested in the realm of rational thought and do not walk by faith but purely by sight. As long as we do not take off these earthly shoes from off our feet and move onto a heavenly ground where we walk by faith and not by sight God will not happen and we will not receive the interpretation of God's will.

Brethren, we who pray the words: "Thy kingdom come, thy will be done in earth, as it is in heaven..." should be very careful. Because for many, God is actually going to respond. God is going to happen. It will come down to being a case of "Let God be true, and every man a liar." Or let every other rational thought, preconceived notion, pre-determined mindset, and opinion, established body of knowledge and experience – let them ALL fade away and let God speak for himself.

Let God be true or be interpreted by his actions. Let God speak by his own actions. Let God manifest his own truth by becoming incarnate in our circumstances. Let God be his own interpreter by whatever and however his ultimate plan and purpose chooses to play out. And we will accept him, we will accept his word, by any means and any manner by which He sees fit to not only release it but also but how He chooses to manifest it. God is his own Divine interpreter.

The grace of our Lord Jesus Christ be with you.

# CHAPTER TWELVE
# IF YE HAD KNOWN ME, YE SHOULD HAVE KNOWN MY FATHER

*"In my Father's house are many mansions: if it were not so, I would have told you. I go to prepare a place for you. And if I go and prepare a place for you, I will come again, and receive you unto myself; that where I am, there ye may be also. And whither I go ye know, and the way ye know. Thomas saith unto him, Lord, we know not whither thou goest; and how can we know the way? Jesus saith unto him, I am the way, the truth, and the life: no man cometh unto the Father, but by me. If ye had known me, ye should have known my Father also: and from henceforth ye know him, and have seen him. Philip saith unto him, Lord, shew us the Father, and it sufficeth us. Jesus saith unto him, Have I been so long time with you, and yet hast thou not known me, Philip? He that hath seen me hath seen the Father."*
*(John 14:2-9)*

The Lord is manifesting in our midst in these end times, but many are unaware of his goings. Many are unaware of the way He is taking... The path He is plying to gather, prepare and bring his

people to the promised land of fullness, of ascendancy in the spiritual and the material world -- in the celestial world and the terrestrial world. A place of peace. A place of harmony between spirit, mind, and body –where we achieve and attain clarity, singularity, and unity with the Spirit of God. Where the words of Isaiah 65:24 become a living reality: "And it shall come to pass, that before they call, I will answer; and while they are yet speaking, I will hear"– because God is fully vested and pleased to dwell within us without measure, even as He did in Christ Jesus.

Because of our inability to fully grasp the shape, form, direction, and visitation of the Christ among us – not as an individualized person, but in terms of the regime and administration of grace, favor and glorious mandates that have been bestowed upon the Church in these last days – we are constantly struggling to utilize, apprehend, possess, and wield the instruments of God's grace and power in any consistent way and manner. Many are bumped and buffeted from pillar to post, from tent to temple and from one Church to another – constantly searching, constantly comparing, and losing faith in this, that or the other. Whereas there is a manifestation of God in and around us that we could learn to tap into, we could learn to adapt to, we could learn to hear, to understand, to correspond with and receive greater faith thereby. And receive spiritual and material benefits and breakthroughs. God is in our midst. God is among us.

Our Lord promised in John 14:18-19 before his departure from his earthly construct: *"I will not leave you comfortless: I will come to you. Yet a little while, and the world seeth me no more; but ye see me: because I live, ye shall live also."*

So, we know that the Lord is still here. Even though we don't readily see him in the natural. He is no less real today than He was two thousand years ago. We just have to attune our senses and antennae to a different set of frequencies in order to communicate with him as effectively as and even more so than was the case when He walked the earth in human form.

Like the disciples initially, we wrestle with the mandates that the Lord requires of us. He expects and requires that we will understand his goings and his visitation, when in fact we mostly don't. When He elaborated on his ascendant path to the fullness of the Godhead on our behalf (i.e., *"I go to the Father"* and *"I go to prepare a place for you"*)

> He would end with the words: *"whither I go ye know, and the way ye know."*

The disciples would come back with: *"Lord, we know not whither thou goest; and how can we know the way?"* This back and forth was almost constant between our Lord and his disciples, and the reason is that the Lord cannot simply tell us things and they will work for us and become a part of us. God is Spirit, and so there is a very large extent to which we must deliberately shift gear by moving our inner man into the Spirit of what God is doing —in order to understand and actualize what in fact God is doing. To experience what God is doing. And so, the Lord would constantly prompt and push his disciples and challenge them to catch the vision of what He was saying or doing.

Hear the Lord in Matt. 16:13 ask the disciples *"Whom do MEN say that I the Son of man am?"* and following their different responses, He now artfully steers them to the question He really meant to ask: *"But whom say YE that I am?"* Peter gives an answer that seems to just 'pop' into his head and heart out of nowhere and in that instant the Lord declares: *"Blessed art thou, Simon Barjona: for flesh and blood hath not revealed it unto thee, but my Father which is in heaven"*, signifying that in that instant, at that moment, Peter made a connection by his inner man with the Spirit of the Father, with the Spirit of God -- through which connection a correct understanding and interpretation of the mystery and the answer to the question was given.

Basically, because of Peter's personal intimacy with Jesus he is able to almost 'telepathically' pull the answer right out from Jesus' (and the Father's) 'thoughts and Spirit.

*The more personally attuned we are to an individual in mind and spirit – be they corporeal or incorporeal – the more we just 'gel', the more we just 'click', the more we catch their drift, their spirit and their essence...*

This is essentially what Jesus meant when He said: *"If ye had known me, ye should have known my Father..."*. This is the key and the practical essence of ascending –of entering into the fuller expanse of the "Father's house" and all it entails in terms of Divine protection and spiritual endowments: we have to work on becoming not just believers in Christ but *friends and intimates* of Jesus Christ. So that we will be constantly, involuntarily, immersed and bathed with the riches of the "Father's house". This is the practical essence of the ascension.

*"Henceforth I call you not servants; for the servant knoweth not what his lord doeth: but I have called you friends; for all things that I have heard of my Father I have made known unto you."* (John 15:15)

## I AM THE WAY, THE TRUTH, AND THE LIFE

(Or to paraphrase: the *Vision*, the *Interpretation,* and the *Fulfillment*)

Our Lord answers the question of *"we know not whither thou goest; and how can we know the way?"* by affirming: *"I am the way, the truth, and the life: no man cometh unto the Father, but by me. If ye had known me, ye should have known my Father also..."*

He is essentially saying He is himself the *vision* or the plan, the details or the *interpretation,* and the *fulfilment* or end-product.

To enjoy the benefits and the fullness of all that has been bequeathed to us (his "Father's house") we have to establish a relationship and ongoing connection with him.

When two people meet for the first time and engage in conversation, there is an almost instant acknowledgement on either side as to the existence (or not) of a kinship of minds and spirits. When it almost seems that we have made this special 'connection' (we've a lot in common, etc.) there is a warming feeling and instant bond that silently says: "we have a lot in common, we need to stay in touch...". That concurrency of the spirit and of the mind that we look for everyday in our relationships with one another is comparable to what the Lord is saying here when He uses the words: *"If ye had known me..."*

If ye had known me... If you had properly understood me... When you are able to come to the place where you are more in harmony, more settled with and more fully comprehend me and the shape, form and nature of how I am currently manifesting in and around you every day -- when you are able to establish the connection with me, that is when you will begin to grasp exactly what and who "the Father" is.

Beyond being a Person in the Godhead, "the Father" symbolizes an entire regime or omnibus appropriations bill laying out citizens' (or saints') rights, benefits and privileges.

*"The Father" represents the ultimate destination, route, and ascension of the creature within the created universe to a place of prosperity. To a place of peace. To a place of harmony and concurrency with the Divine...*

To a place where there is no sickness and no disease. A place where death has no say and no sway. A place where demons have not the right of way. A place where there is victory and where God's original thought and intention for man is being realized. That is what Jesus labored to explain to the disciples. Connect with me on that spiritual level and you will know or experience the Father, i.e. you will have access and rights to the vast store and preserve of grace, healing, victory, and favor.

The woman with the issue of blood 12 years felt *unworthy* to approach Jesus or his disciples (this important fact is often ignored when references are made to her faith alone). As a result, and in that state of mind and spirit (i.e., *"The LORD is nigh unto them that are of a broken heart; and saveth such as be of a contrite spirit."* Psalm 34:18), she said within herself: *"If I can just touch the hem of his garment I shall be healed..."* In that instant, she made the correct connection with the Lord based on her faith and the state of her heart, her spirit. She 'spoke' in God's language, she spoke directly into the Spirit of Jesus –and as a result, even though Jesus did not physically pray for her or address himself to her she received riches of healing and miracle from the "Father's house".

Do you get it?

For all intents and purposes, Jesus may not have been there *physically* (as is the case with us now and with his disciples after his resurrection and ascension). He might as well not have been there physically, because her view of him (and his of her) was obscured by the crowd –hence his question: "Who touched me?" Notwithstanding the Lord's 'physical absence' (as it were), all she needed was a point of reference for her faith to activate the invisible prophetic (almost 'telepathic') connection with him to release the miracle – *"If I can just touch the hem of his garment..."*.

In another instance, a Roman soldier had spoken to our Lord about his servant who was ill. As our Lord made to follow him and physically attend to his servant the soldier forbad him, essentially saying he "understood" the Lord for who He was and since he (the soldier) considered himself *unworthy* (again, an element often ignored when reference is made to his faith) for

Jesus to come into his abode all Jesus needed to do was say the word and his servant would be healed. As was the case of the woman with an issue of blood, Jesus did not *physically* pray for or attend the sick person, yet both the sick individual and his proxy witnessed a miraculous intervention from God.

And so, when Jesus is saying to his disciples: *"And whither I go ye know, and the way ye know..."*, He is saying that having witnessed all those examples of how people 'entered' his "Father's house" and took the blessings (i.e. miracles and healings) that they wanted or needed –the disciples already understood the principle of utilizing the glories and benefits of the Father's house by making that 'connection' with him on a non-corporeal level; i.e. on a level that is irrespective of his *physical* presence or absence. Elsewhere, we read the account of how, using the same principle of the non-corporeal or non-physical connection, Jesus upbraided Thomas for his unbelief: *"Jesus saith unto him, Thomas, because thou hast seen me, thou hast believed: blessed are they that have not seen, and yet have believed."*

In other words, "blessed" is he (i.e., he has 'won the jackpot' or 'won the lottery') who has learned the principle of walking straight into "the Father's house" by having the right attitude and with faith *without* relying on the *physical* senses (i.e., the physical or visible presence of our Lord).

There is more power to be gleaned and appropriated by this method of seeing without having seen. It also explains the Lord's words when He said: *"he that believeth on me, the works that I do shall he do also; and greater works than these shall he do; because I go to my Father"* (i.e., I go into Spirit form; from corporeal to non-corporeal, from physical to spiritual --to become the CEO of the Father's glorious estate of blessings on behalf of the saints).

## DON'T BE DISTRACTED BY THE FLESH

*"Thomas saith unto him, Lord, we know not whither thou goest; and how can we know the way?... Philip saith unto him, Lord, shew us the Father, and it sufficeth us. Jesus saith unto him, Have I been so long time with you, and yet hast thou not known me, Philip?"*

Our biggest distraction to properly harnessing the power that is within and around us and is manifesting in our midst in these end times is the flesh, i.e., what we *readily* see and what we *don't readily* see. Or the question of 'how' we see something, or why God should show us something one way and not the other way (that we are accustomed to or have been taught or orientated by) –or why what God is doing or saying doesn't leap out at us (in the nature of a 'headliner') and grab our attention as we are accustomed to in today's non-subtle world of verbose and noisy multimedia applications , advertising and messaging. Why God's movement and direction is so subtle and requiring that we 'pay attention' and remain attuned to his 'channel', etc.

The Lord says:

*"Come to understand ME more fully in terms of how I am evolving and have evolved – from the natural to something more, something different -- then you will begin to come into the good and the awareness and realization of WHO and*

*WHAT the Father is. You will experience what it means to be one with me and with the Father. And in that three-way triangle of correspondence, "At that day ye shall know that I am in my Father, and ye in me, and I in you." (John 14:20): the works that I do you will understand HOW they are possible, and yourself by yourself be able to do even GREATER works than I have done."*

*"Verily, verily, I say unto you, He that believeth on me, the works that I do shall he do also; and greater works than these shall he do; because I go unto my Father. And whatsoever ye shall ask in my name, that will I do, that the Father may be glorified in the Son. If ye shall ask any thing in my name, I will do it."* (John 14:12-13)

As we legitimately seek to avail ourselves of the blessings and the grace of God in its many and varied forms – be it in the areas of healing, financial and other kinds of breakthrough, deliverance and victory – we need to also be careful to situate ourselves in that place or in those places where we can be taught and ushered towards a fuller grasp, understanding and realization of what is Christ's incumbent, unfolding plan and agenda for the Lord's people in these last days. Our Lord said: *"If ye had known me, ye should have known my father also."*

So, understanding how the Lord is manifesting in our times, in our day and in our lives is key to the experience of God, is key to a greater harmony and oneness with the Spirit of God – which is the route to power and to the miraculous. This is the sure route to the supernatural. Where we are no longer running to and fro seeking whom to pray for us, but we can pray ourselves and for others and get results.

## THE RIGHT ATTITUDE (CONTRITION AND HUMILITY) WITH FAITH TRANSCENDS THE PHYSICAL DIMENSION AND TOUCHES OTHER DIMENSIONS BESIDES THE PHYSICAL

Place your hand near -- or touch -- a pot or kettle of freshly made coffee and you can feel the heat emanating from it. In the instant that your hand receives the acute sensation of heat both you and the pot of boiling liquid have established a connection whereby the transfer of energy occurs between the one and the other. If you draw your hand away the connection is degraded in intensity, and you feel less of the warmness of the pot. If you exit the room where the pot rests on the table and upon entering a different room, you wave your hand around you feel none of the warmth and heat from the pot because you are physically removed from proximity to it and as such you cannot pick up any of the sensations of heat or warmth from the pot.

When you walk into the grocery store and move toward the cold cuts and meats section you immediately get the sensation of increased coldness because of your proximity to the cuts displayed on ice or on the frigid meat bays. As you move farther away from those bays and the meat section in general you get less of the sensation of coldness because you have become physically distanced from the focal point from which the cold sensation emanated.

So, there are elements and energies that we can sense, with which we can connect, purely based on *physical* proximity – though we may or may not *physically* touch the objects that host those energies. The mere fact that we are within close enough proximity to the host or endpoint ensures that we receive a sensation, because the elements and energies belong to the same dimension: the *physical* dimension.

However, there are elemental forces and energies that we sense every day, that exercise very strong influences over our lives and in many cases even control us – which emanate from objects that we *do not* approximate in a *physical* way. Nevertheless, we can sense or establish a connection with these energies to the extent that there is a *real* correspondence with the host objects or endpoints. There is a level of 'understanding' and a 'perception' that exists between the one and the other. Many times, there is even concurrency or harmony of ideas, of purpose, desire, and expectation between the one and the other. We describe this phenomenon and certain aspects of it by using words like *intuition, premonition, sixth sense,* etc. There are other words that may be used to describe aspects of this phenomenon.

How is it, for instance, that we feel the strings of love for another even though we cannot *physically* see the person? When we share affection with another, you would think (as with the pot of boiling coffee) that as we separate and move away from each other we will get less of the sensation of love between us – that we will no longer feel the 'heat' or 'warmth' of our shared love and affection because we are physically dispersed from one another. You would think that it would be impossible to still make the 'connection' by which this sensation of the strangely powerful and captivating energy called love may travel.

Now, in time this connection may grow weaker – until it is no longer there, and we feel no 'strings' as it were pulling at us from across the physical divide (be it a year or more of separation across two towns, two states, or two countries). That is understandable, as sensation – even physical sensation – can wear off with time, misuse, and abuse. However, in many instances rather than grow weaker due to physical dispersion the love grows stronger. We find that love is still felt (i.e., you still get the sensation strong as ever) even after death and beyond the grave. Many are unable to pull themselves together even after several months and years of a departed one's decease and sometimes even take their own lives – to go and meet their dearly beloved departed. Love is a force, an energy that lives in more than one dimension besides just the physical but is no less strong and is in fact stronger than sensations that are local to the physical dimension alone.

How is it possible that we can still feel the cords of love so strong for one who has departed this physical life – and vice-versa -- where we observe that frequently the soul of a departed will visit those whom they loved and left behind in their dreams or by other unexplainable paranormal and psychic phenomena? How is this possible? If not, that love is a force that transcends dimensions and is not limited to one dimension only? Love reaches across the divide, through the curtain that separates the physical from the spiritual. Make no mistake, love is a living active force or energy that compels and controls. It is very powerful, oftentimes too powerful for some.

Another strong sensation that is possible to feel despite being physically dispersed from somebody else is hate. Just like you can feel when somebody you love or by whom you are loved enters a room and you raise your head or look around you involuntarily to catch a glimpse of them, so also it is possible to get the sensation of hate or ill-will when a person enters or passes through a room. So also, it is possible to get the sensation of fear in the same, similar, and other ways. The Bible refers to a "spirit of fear" because fear operates in and transcends the physical too, onto the spiritual spheres.

Love, hope, hate, fear (and others) are energies that transcend the physical into the spiritual dimension –a dimension traversed by spirit and not by flesh. This is why it is common to have dreams of people that love you or that hate you, or dreams of people whom you fear (for whatever reason) – because those energies travel in the spiritual dimension. They are not limited or restricted by the physical or by physical circumstances. They appertain to the spirit and to the mind (soul).

There is another energy or element of the soul and the spirit of man that transcends physical dimensions, and that is faith. Real, tangible faith is an attitude of the heart. It is the hidden, invisible, relationship and correspondence between the unworthy supplicant and their benefactor in Heaven. That hidden, invisible 'correspondence' is what the Bible describes as *"the substance of things hoped for, the evidence of things not seen"* (Hebrews 11:1). Our Lord labored to teach us valuable lessons on faith to enable us enjoy a rich and meaningful relationship with him.

There is a realm of correspondence with "the Father", of concurrency of thought, ideas, and purpose with God --very similar to the correspondence that occurs between persons that share love and affection -- that is unaffected by geography or the fact we dwell natively in the natural and God dwells natively in the spiritual world. This ability to make a 'connection' with God on another level and – on the one hand – receive messaging from him without necessarily hearing an *audible* voice in the natural (as did Peter when our Lord commended him for *hearing* clearly from "the Father" in Heaven in Matt. 16:13-17) and on the other hand, send a *verbally unspoken* request to God and get an answer without making physical contact with or being spoken to or prayed for by anyone (as did the woman healed of an issue of blood in Matthew 9:21) --is *faith*. Faith transcends dimensions, Faith is the ability to make the connection with the God who is invisible and establish a correspondence with Him where we are at once in-sync with Him and can communicate *non-verbally*, but *intuitively*, *natively* within our spirit man – with the God who is himself Spirit.

This is in fact the way that we ought to communicate and correspond with (or worship) God:

> *"God is a Spirit: and they that worship him must worship him in spirit and in truth."* (John 4:24)

This kind of "faith" is what we are supposed to exercise in these days to establish an increasingly intense familiarity and intimacy with the Lord Jesus Christ who has passed into the realm of invisibility to the natural, but visibility to the spiritual minded and spiritual conscious. Our Lord is very much among us, having only changed his *presence-with- us* (i.e., "Emmanuel") or his *protocol* (for communication) from flesh to Spirit...

*"And I will pray the Father, and he shall give you another Comforter, that he may abide with you for ever; Even the Spirit of truth; whom the world cannot receive, because it seeth him not, neither knoweth him: but YE KNOW HIM; for he dwelleth WITH YOU, and shall be IN YOU. I WILL NOT LEAVE you comfortless: I WILL COME to you. Yet a little while, and the world seeth ME NO MORE; but YE SEE ME: because I live, ye shall live also."* (John 14:16-19)

We need to get used to him – in this form. We need to become familiar with him – in this form. We need learn how to relate with and correspond with him – in this form. More than that, we need to become *friends of Jesus* –not just born-again believers. This is the *key* to enjoying the benefits and *ascending* to the rights and privileges of "the Father's house." So that the vast riches and wealth that are the fullness of "the Father's house" (knowledge, wisdom, miracles, healing, increase, breakthroughs, and deliverance of all sorts) might become our portion and we might appropriate, wear and utilize them while in the body and through this channel. This is what He meant when He said:

*"If ye had known me, ye should have known my Father also"*
*(John 8:19; 14:7)*

The nature of Christianity is not for the Lord's people to be running about in search of healing. Healing is the children's bread (Matt. 15:21- 28). But for many, we are not yet at the point where we are able to fully utilize this aspect of "the Father's house". Whereas the world should be trooping to the Church to receive healing and not vice versa. Divine healing should not be something that is abused as a basis for extortion from hapless supplicants. Healing should abound and be freely experienced within the churches, while those who are more mature are breaking ground and laying the foundations for weightier things, i.e. Resurrection, Ascension and Rapture. This is consistent with the words of Apostle Paul in Philippians 3:10-16 and particularly verses 15 and where he said concerning the pursuit of resurrection power:

*"Let us therefore, as many as be perfect (i.e. mature), be thus minded: and if in any thing ye be otherwise minded, God shall reveal even this unto you. Nevertheless, whereto we have already attained, let us walk by the same rule, let us mind the same thing."*

There is an Open Heaven that the Lord is unveiling in these days, and it is knocking at the door and beckoning on many, some of whom barely realize it. Many doors have been opened in the past. But a new suite of doors is being opened in our days. We will have to learn to see and hear through these new doors all at once without preferring one above the other. This is a path through which the Lord is going to unveil himself to his chosen in these last days. If ye had known me, ye should have known my Father...

We are going to have to do the hard work of getting to know the Lord better. Getting to understand how to relate with him better. Getting to attain a higher level or degree of harmony with him and with the Holy Spirit – in order that we will get to KNOW THE FATHER and be clothed, endowed and have capacity to utilize freely and easily the full scope of blessings, grace, power and benefits that are ours within our "Father's house," where there is prepared for each one of the Lord's people their own special place and their own unique situation.

*"He that hath an ear, let him hear what the Spirit saith unto the churches; To him that overcometh will I give to eat of the hidden manna, and will give him a white stone, and in the stone a new name written, which no man knoweth saving he that receiveth it."*

The grace of our Lord Jesus Christ be with you all.

# ABOUT THE AUTHOR

Kevin has dedicated his life to preaching and teaching the Gospel of Jesus Christ, which he has done to peoples, communities, and churches across the globe since he was a boy. His Messenger Series books reveal and teach elements of the deeper Christian life and devotion to God. Kevin's church mission outreach based in Garland, Texas, U.S.A. is Spoken Word Faith Ministries.